family circle®

Party & Finger Food

The Family Circle® Promise of Success

Welcome to the world of Confident Cooking,
created for you in the Australian **Family Circle®
Test Kitchen,** where recipes are double-tested by
our team of home economists to achieve a
high standard of success—and delicious
results every time. For UK conversions and a glossary
explaining unfamiliar terms see page 112.

MURDOCH BOOKS®
Sydney • London • Vancouver • New York

C O N T E

Caesar Salad, page 69.

Smoked Cod and Spinach Roulade, page 59.

Prawn Toasts, page 41.

Apple Lemon Bavarois with Toffee, page 80.

Marbled Blueberry Cake, page 92.

Pistachio Praline Truffles, page 105.

The Publisher thanks the following for their assistance in the photography for this book: Limogue Australia, Country Affair, L.A. Design, Antico's Fruitworld, Doug Piper's Butchery, Corso di Fiori, De Costi's Seafood, Zuhaus/Butler and Co, Morris Home and Garden Wares, Home and Garden on the Mall, Waterford Wedgwood, Royal Doulton, Villeroy & Boch, Cydonia, The Glass Studio, Euroespresso, Wardlaw Fabrics, The Natural Floorcovering Centre, Grange Furniture, St James Furnishings.

Herbed Fillet of Beef, page 57.

The test kitchen where our recipes are double-tested by our team of home economists to achieve a high standard of success and delicious results every time.

When we test our recipes, we rate them for ease of preparation. The following cookery ratings are on the recipes in this book, making them easy to use and understand.

A single Cooking with Confidence symbol indicates a recipe that is simple and generally quick to make – perfect for beginners.

Two symbols indicate the need for just a little more care and a little more time.

Three symbols indicate special dishes that need more investment in time, care and patience – but the results are worth it.

Front cover: A tempting array of party foods featured in the book.
Inside front cover: Apple and Sultana Brandied Bread Pudding (top) and Lemon Passionfruit Syllabub with Berries, page 84.

Planning a Party

A successful party is one where everyone feels welcome and comfortable, and where the hosts have as much fun as their guests. The secret, even for the most informal gathering, is in the *planning*—right down to the last detail.

The party plan

When throwing a party, attention to detail will make the difference between an unforgettable event and an ordinary one. Making lists of things to do and what to buy cuts down on panic, makes sure nothing is forgotten, helps keep costs down and allows you to relax on the day.

Spend plenty of time planning your party, aiming for a balance between last-minute preparations and things that can be done ahead, especially when it comes to the food.

Food and drink form the heart of a good party, but they are not the only things you will need to think about.

Golden rules

• Minimise last-minute preparations or serving so that you can be with your guests. Design things so that everyone can enjoy themselves fully on the day.
• Don't try to do it all on your own — enlist help and delegate jobs.
• Make party preparations fun.

First things

To plan your party, ask yourself the following questions:

1. What type of party is it?

Is it being held to celebrate a special occasion? Will it have a theme? Do you want it to be casual or formal, large or intimate, simple or lavish? Will it be held outdoors, indoors or a combination of both? Is it going to involve a sit-down dinner, buffet, or just drinks and nibbles ?

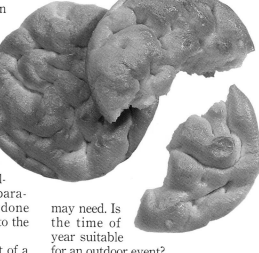

2. When will it be held?

The season will influence your choice of venue and the menu, as well as the equipment you may need. Is the time of year suitable for an outdoor event? Decide how long you want the party to last— a few hours, all night or even all weekend.

3. Where will you hold it?

Is there enough room for your guests to be comfortable? Check especially whether bathroom facilities can cope with the number of guests. If an outdoor party is planned, have a contingency plan for wet weather.

4. How many guests do you want to invite?

Unless the occasion (such as an important family milestone) dictates the guest list, invite numbers your resources can cope with. Consider what the venue can accommodate and decide whether that will determine guest numbers. If your guest list is invariable, you may have to consider alternative venues.

Take account of what the kitchen and equipment can cope with. Think about how many helping hands you can pay—or persuade—to contribute to the effort.

Most importantly, consider what your budget will stretch to.

5. How much can you spend?

Party costs can include:
• Food
• Drink
• Extra supplies such as garbage bags, disposable party ware, bathroom needs, food wrap
• Decorations
• Venue hire
• Equipment hire
• Hired help
• Entertainment costs
• Invitations

When drawing up your budget, include everything you think you will need and then cut back to essentials if necessary. Decide on the most important element of your party—the food, drinks, entertainment or an unusual setting—and concentrate your resources on this aspect.

Invitations

Give plenty of notice (say two weeks to a month) when inviting people to your party. For all but the most formal of occasions, telephoning is simpler. Indicate the kind of party—tell guests if dinner is being served, and how formal an occasion it is to be as a guide to dress.

Give clear directions to the venue and let your guests know about parking posssibilities, especially if you are expecting large numbers.

Ask for firm responses to help you plan the catering.

Getting help

For more than about 20 guests at anything but the most informal drinks party, it may be worthwhile hiring help in the form of waiters, a bar person, or even a maid or assistant cook. Alternatively, you could recruit willing members of the family or friends.

Delegate responsibilities clearly and make sure everyone understands his or her roles. Organise helpers on the day and assign tasks clearly, especially around the kitchen.

Get quotes from a number of firms if you are hiring equipment or people. Ask friends to recommend a reputable source, or look in the yellow pages and

Equipment checklist

If you are borrowing equipment, make sure that it will be available on the day. Hire anything you need well in advance and have it delivered the day before.

- [ ] Lots of airtight storage containers of varying sizes
- [ ] Fridge and/or freezer space for prepared food and ingredients
- [ ] Fridge space/plastic garbage bins to take ice for drinks
- [ ] Portable ice boxes for extra food storage on the day
- [ ] Attractive (but not so fussy as to detract from the food), durable platters, serving bowls and utensils, punch bowl
- [ ] China and glassware
- [ ] Cutlery
- [ ] Extra hotplates
- [ ] Microwave oven
- [ ] Trestle tables for extra work surfaces or for serving food
- [ ] Chafing dishes
- [ ] Casserole dishes, tureens
- [ ] Baking dishes and trays
- [ ] Hot water urn
- [ ] A trolley or serving cart
- [ ] Small tables placed strategically to accommodate guests' glasses, ashtrays and plates of food
- [ ] Trays
- [ ] Coasters or some kind of protection for good furniture surfaces
- [ ] Enough ashtrays
- [ ] Disposable party ware (cups, plates, napkins etc), if using
- [ ] Chairs, tables for seating guests
- [ ] Linen
- [ ] Tent or marquee
- [ ] Dance floor
- [ ] Extra heating or cooling equipment
- [ ] Sound system or jukebox
- [ ] Christmas or fairy lights, lanterns, garden flares

phone catering services and employment agencies. Student children of friends may be glad of the opportunity to earn some money, and often have waiting or bartending experience. Hospitality training schools may also hire out their students.

Once you have decided on staff, agree on hours, remuneration and payment arrangements, as well as responsibilities on the night. Arrange for hired help to arrive in plenty of time to be briefed on the number of guests you are expecting and the timetable for service, and make sure they are shown kitchen facilities, location of equipment and supplies, and the venue's layout.

The food

When deciding on the food, be practical as well as imaginative. It needs to be manageable if guests are standing (bite-size finger foods, not crumbly or dripping with sauces). The food served should offer your guests variety and choice—a lively balance of strong and mild flavours, savoury, sweet, hot and cold items, rich and light foods, different textures and colours. For a party, especially, presentation is as important as flavour.

Party food should be nutritious and satisfying, as well as exciting. The type and quantities of food to serve will depend on the type of party, season, time of day or night and duration of the party, as well as guest numbers.

Provide some vegetarian options, unless all your guests are meat-eaters.

As a guide for a buffet, provide hot dishes, platters of cold meat, seafood and/or poultry, a selection of salads (the number will depend on whether you serve hot vegetables), two or three desserts, fresh fruit, cheeses and appetisers. Sauces, dips, side dishes and some interesting breads will allow guests to dress up their own selections.

Estimate quantities according to number of guests and how long the party is expected to last. People generally eat more if the weather is cold, and you will need more food for an all-night party than for a 3-hour drinks gathering. Plan for back-up food in case of unexpectedly large appetites.

Also make sure your guests know that food will be served so they do not eat beforehand and leave your culinary masterpieces untouched.

Be realistic about your cooking abilities and don't try out unfamiliar or tricky techniques on the day of the party—it will only cause anxiety and a failed dish will be demoralising.

Time savers and shortcuts

Parties are possible for even the most casual of cooks. When planning the food, decide what to make and what to buy. Prepare some food in advance and freeze it. Take advantage of pre-prepared items now available from delicatessens and butchers. Cold and marinated meats, seafood and poultry can be bought and adapted as the basis of spectacular festive platters. Different olives and cheeses as well as snacks like dolmades make suitable hors d'oeuvres. Simple but exotic dips like taramasalata and hummus can be purchased if you are pressed for time; present them in pretty serving bowls. Add garnishes and accompaniments like breads, crisp vegetable crudités and crackers.

Use bottled and pre-prepared ingredients where possible to save time. Check your pantry before you start cooking to see if essential items need replenishing.

Pastry shells and other baked goods plus some fillings and sauces can be cooked up to a week in advance and frozen. Pastry dough can be prepared and frozen.

The day before, prepare and refrigerate or store foods such as marinated meats, poultry and coffee accompaniments. Make sure you have a good supply of airtight containers, as well as microwave-safe dishes and bowls.

A microwave is a great time-saver for both preparing and reheating party food. If you don't have one, see if you can borrow one.

Place coffee (and tea) supplies in a separate area, ready to be served. Check that you have adequate coffee- and tea-making equipment and supplies, and enough cups or mugs.

Drinks

Decide whether you will have a drinks waiter or a bartender, or allow guests to get their own drinks.

Estimate the quantities of beer, wine, spirits and mixers you will need. Even if you are throwing a casual BYO party, you will still need to buy some alcohol.

Keep in mind the weather and setting when planning drinks, and include plenty of fruit juices, mineral water and soft drinks.

Check that equipment (blenders, cocktail shakers, strainers, a range of glasses, etc) is available if cocktails are to be served.

Stock up on ingredients to make punch or sangria (mulled wine is nice for winter).

Decide whether you need to hire or borrow extra glasses. Add ice and garnishes to your shopping list. Check your fridge capacity and estimate the amount of ice and 'ice buckets' (large plastic garbage bins are good) you will need to cope with any overflow.

Setting the scene

If you are holding your party at home, make imaginative use of attractive garden settings if weather permits. Consider terraces, garage or basement areas, as well as the house. Serve drinks in one area and food in another.

Put some thought into decorations or props to set the tone of your party and give it an individual stamp. They can be simple or elaborate, depending on the type of party and your budget, reflecting the season, the theme of the party or the reason for holding it.

If you are making your own decorations, allow plenty of time. Make it fun and enlist help from family or friends.

Flowers are always effective and a single large centrepiece will have more impact than several small displays. Flowers in the bathroom are nice.

Table centrepieces can be made from unusual objects, bowls or baskets of fruit tied with ribbon, garden greenery, potted plants, attractive vegetables (shiny eggplants, glowing pumpkins, bright asparagus).

Place flowers and candles where they will be noticed but not get in the way. Check that you have suitable vases and candle holders.

Helium-filled balloons, streamers or other novelties can add a sense of fun.

Rearrange (or temporarily store) furniture to make space if necessary;

remove or cover anything you don't want damaged by cigarettes, alcohol, food spillages or other accidents. Protect carpet with old rugs or by rolling them up.

Put up signs to direct guests to the bathroom and 'cloakroom' areas if there is likely to be confusion. Set aside a space for belongings which is out of the way and safe.

Provide extra supplies (toilet paper, tissues, soap, hand-towels).

Decide whether smoking will be restricted to certain areas.

Check that there is plenty of seating if it is to be a lengthy party (have some folding chairs in reserve), and that the venue will not be too warm or too cold.

Lighting should be neither too dim nor too bright. Use candles for added atmosphere. Arrange lighting and lamps to highlight entrances and areas you want noticed (like food tables), making sure stairs or dark corridors are well lit to head off accidents. For outdoor settings, try garden flares or kerosene lanterns, making sure they are clear of trees or any flammable structures. If setting up lights outdoors, ensure any electrical leads are out of the way or securely taped down.

Assign collection points for rubbish and provide bins. Guests can make cleaning up easier if they know where to dispose of their leftovers, beer cans, cigarettes and other rubbish.

If it is a very special occasion, you may also want to hire a photographer.

Music

Decide on the music for your party well in advance. Choose carefully to suit the mood you want to create—a mix of relaxing and energetic styles to vary the tempo is a good idea—and take into account whether there is likely to be dancing.

If booking musicians or a singer, or hiring a DJ, make sure you are happy with the style of music they plan to play and that your guests will enjoy it. Also agree beforehand on how long musicians will play.

If you are using your own sound system, decide whether it needs to be moved or rearranged. You may have to boost its capabilities by hiring (or borrowing) extra components from a trusting friend. Test the system before the night.

If you are entrusting your sound system to your guests, make tapes accessible and clearly label them. Decide who will be in charge of maintaining the mood and momentum if you do not want chaos.

Sanity savers

Do not schedule your party for a busy or stressful time. Keep up your regular routine as much as possible.

Delegate—do yourself only what you are most confident about and good at. Accept offers of help and ask for it; give people jobs they will enjoy—

playing bar-person, doing the garden, choosing and arranging flowers, recording music.

Trusting anything to memory is asking for trouble. Put up shopping lists, timetables and to-do lists in prominent places—everyone will feel happier if jobs are ticked off the list when completed.

Make comprehensive shopping lists and review often to minimise last minute panics. Divide the shopping between helpers.

Make sure you check in advance with suppliers on any difficult to get or unusual items.

Stock up on the essentials, including clear food wrap, aluminium foil, garbage bags, paper towels, matches, toothpicks, paper napkins, cocktail sticks, paper towels and extra bathroom supplies.

Stretch your budget by shopping at fresh produce markets (fruit, vegetables, fish, wholesale delicatessen outlets and meat suppliers) if you can.

Pre-cook food. Hire or borrow equipment and helpers. Have a clear budget, with a little in reserve for emergencies, and stick to it. Be realistic about your resources (time, money, space). Don't be over-ambitious: guests will not judge your party by how extravagant you are but by how much care and thought you have put into entertaining them.

Make sure your guests know about any wet weather arrangements.

Tell the neighbours about the party (invite them if it's appropriate), and inform yourself about the noise laws in your area.

Anticipate problems—there will always be a few disasters, but any party can survive dishes that did not work out, unco-operative weather or unexpected demands on the food and drink, provided you have planned ahead. It helps to have a sense of humour, and remember that the purpose of throwing a party is not to impress, but for everyone to enjoy themselves—especially you.

Party timetable

1. Weeks ahead:
☐ Make up the guestlist, invite people and get firm responses;
☐ Plan food, drink, decorations;
☐ Choose recipes, noting the time they will take, any equipment you do not already have on hand, and whether they fit in with your overall menu plan;
☐ Write shopping lists;
☐ Draw up a list of things to do and a timetable for the weeks/days leading up to the party, and for the day after. Make a time-line right up to the day after the party, taking into account the need to return equiment, put furniture back into place and pay any hired staff. Include a plan for cleaning up and who is going to do it. Put the timetable for the day of the party on prominent display on a wall or notice board;
☐ Recruit helpers; arrange hire of waiters etc;
☐ List any extra equipment you will need and arrange to borrow or hire it;
☐ Shop for drinks and non-perisable supplies, including party accessories and decorations;
☐ Place any large orders for meat and other supplies;
☐ Book entertainment or choose music and make tapes;

2. Days ahead:
☐ Check and buy any supplies you have forgotten, including drinks;
☐ Cook food that can be frozen or stored;
☐ Clean the venue (including outdoor areas);
☐ Take delivery of hired equipment; pick up any items you are borrowing.;

3. The day before:
☐ Do final cleaning jobs; tidy garden and house;
☐ Make space in refrigerator(s);
☐ Freeze ice cubes;
☐ Clear space for supplies;
☐ Shop for fresh fruit, vegetables for salads, meat and poultry;
☐ Decorate venue (except for flowers). Arrange the space: move furniture, place buffet tables so that guests have enough room to serve themselves;
☐ Set up dessert and coffee area;
☐ Set tables, place ashtrays; set up the bar;
☐ Check drinks supplies and refrigerate;
☐ Thaw frozen items overnight;

4. Hours ahead/on the day:
☐ Shop early for flowers, fresh seafood, bread and anything else you have forgotten;
☐ Prepare garnishes (eg lemon wedges, parsley, dill, watercress, cherry tomatoes, shallots, chives, colourful peppers, zuchini and carrot slices, bunches of grapes, strawberries, fresh vine leaves);
☐ Assemble food (leave reheating until last), do remaining cooking;
☐ Unmould dishes that need care (pates, terrines, galantines);
☐ Clear work surfaces;
☐ Double check that you have all necessary ingredients on hand. If you have forgotten something, ask a helper to get it for you;
☐ Lay out serving dishes and platers (use unusual shapes, large rather than small, colourful, baskets, wooden trays or boards) and make sure there are enough. When setting out the food, arrange it in a logical order for serving, and keep a little in reserve for latecomers;
☐ Prepare coffee pots or have tea and coffee things set up;
☐ If hiring help, confirm their time of arrival;
☐ If the party is being held in your home, make sure it is well-aired and not filled with cooking odours;
☐ Put an ashtray in the bathroom;
☐ Clean up any disasters and forget about them;
☐ Have a helper collect ice an hour or so before the party is scheduled to begin;
☐ Allow an hour or two to relax before your guests arrive, and dress yourself as though you are going to a party.

PARTY SHORTCUTS

Take the panic out of party-giving with some food and drink shortcuts that still produce festive results. You can put together a party in no time—all it takes is a little imagination and some clever shopping.

Punches

BRANDY ALEXANDER PUNCH

Combine 750 ml brandy, 375 ml crème de cacao and 600 ml cream in a large bowl or jug. Whisk until ingredients are well combined. Place some ice in a large punch bowl and pour the cream mixture over the top. Sprinkle with nutmeg before serving.

PIMM'S PUNCH

Place some ice into a large punch bowl or jug. Add 375 ml each of Pimm's No. 1 and Southern Comfort, 180 ml sweet vermouth, 180 ml dark rum (not overproof), 375 ml orange juice, 750 ml champagne, one 250 g punnet strawberries, hulled and sliced, plus a few orange, lime and lemon slices. Add some fresh peeled and sliced ripe mango, if desired, for a tropical touch. Mix well and serve punch immediately.

PINEAPPLE AND PASSIONFRUIT PUNCH

Combine 2 cups strong hot black tea with 1/4 cup demerara sugar in a medium bowl. Stir until the sugar has dissolved. Cool.

Place 3/4 cup lemon juice, 4 cups pineapple juice, 1–2 tablespoons lime cordial, 1.25 ml bottle soda water, 2 1.25 ml bottles lemonade, one 425 g can crushed pineapple, the cooled tea and the pulp of 5 passionfruit in a large punch bowl. Mix well. Add some crushed ice, shredded fresh mint and orange slices and serve. As a variation, a few drops of Angostura bitters may be added.

Note: For a quick, refreshing punch, combine some fresh chopped fruits, a little sugar, champagne and ice in a blender. Process until smooth. Serve immediately. To make a non-alcoholic version, omit the champagne and add fruit juice instead.

Pimm's Punch (far left), Brandy Alexander Punch (centre) and Pineapple Passionfruit Punch.

The Deli Plate

Creating an exciting deli plate is a simple and fuss-free way of entertaining. Combine the flavours of different cheeses with some marinated olives, mushrooms and artichokes, cured, smoked or spicy meats, succulent dried and fresh fruits, and a variety of biscuits and wafers. A presentation made up of simple ingredients like these will tempt any palate.

Choose a range of cheeses—at least three. Serve one hard or firm cheese, such as a vintage or tasty cheddar, edam, gouda, jarslberg, tilsit, port salut, leicester, or your own favourite; a soft cheese like camembert, brie, havarti, bocconcini, feta, ricotta or a soft blue cheese; and one other, perhaps from the large variety of fruit, pepper or herb cheeses available.

Marinated olives, mushrooms and artichokes are always popular. These can be purchased already prepared, leaving the cook with very little to do. Or create your own, following our quick one-step recipes.

Meats such as salami, pastrami, prosciutto, mortadella, pepperoni, ham and pâtés make tantalising party fare. They team spectacularly with fruits like melon and grapes, and fresh or dried apricots, pears and figs.

MARINATED MUSHROOMS

Combine 2 tablespoons each lemon juice and oil, 2 teaspoons soft brown sugar, 1 tablespoon each chopped fresh mint and parsley, 1 clove crushed garlic, salt and pepper in a medium bowl. Mix well. Stir in 300 g baby button mushrooms. Toss well. Cover and refrigerate 2–3 hours or until mushrooms are slightly softened.

MARINATED ARTICHOKES

Combine 1 tablespoon chopped fresh lemon thyme, 1 tablespoon white wine vinegar, 2 tablespoons olive oil, 1 clove crushed garlic (optional), 1/2 teaspoon grated lime or lemon rind, salt and 1 teaspoon dried crushed pink peppercorns in a medium bowl. Mix well. Stir in 410 g can or jar artichoke hearts, drained and halved. Toss well. Let stand 2–3 hours.

MARINATED FETA CHEESE

Combine 1/4 cup mustard seed oil, 1 teaspoon grated lemon rind, 1 teaspoon each chopped chives, marjoram and tarragon, 1/4 teaspoon dried chilli flakes, 1/4 teaspoon garam masala and some freshly cracked black pepper in a medium bowl. Mix well. Toss through 300 g feta cheese cut into 1.5 cm cubes. Cover and refrigerate for up to 2 hours.

CHILLI HERB OLIVES

Combine in medium bowl 1/4 cup good olive oil, 1/2–1 teaspoon finely chopped red chilli, 1 clove crushed garlic, 1 tablespoon balsamic vinegar, 2 teaspoons each of chopped fresh oregano, basil and chives, salt and freshly ground black pepper. Mix well. Stir in 1 cup whole black or green olives. Toss until well combined. Cover and stand for up to 1 hour or more to allow flavours to develop.

*Clockwise
from right:
Chilli Herb Olives;
Marinated Artichokes;
Chilli Crusted Salami;
Marinated Feta Cheese;
Camembert; Tilsit Cheese
and Marinated Mushrooms.*

The 10-minute Party

GINGER SOY OYSTERS

Combine in small bowl 2 tablespoons each soy sauce and sweet sherry, 3 teaspoons sesame oil, 1 tablespoon finely shredded ginger, 1 spring onion cut into long shreds, and freshly ground pepper. Place 1½ dozen oysters on oven tray. Spoon mixture evenly over each oyster. Bake in preheated moderate 180°C oven 5–10 minutes, or until oysters are cooked through. Transfer to serving platter.

ORANGE GLAZED BARBECUED CHICKEN

Combine ¼ cup orange marmalade, 20 g butter, 1 tablespoon soy sauce, 2 teaspoons sesame oil, salt and pepper in a small pan. Stir over low heat until ingredients are well combined and heated through. Place 1–2 barbecued chickens in a large baking dish. Brush well with marmalade mixture. Bake in preheated moderately slow 160°C oven 15–20 minutes or until chicken is heated through. (To prevent chicken drying out or burning, cover with foil halfway through cooking.) Cut chicken into serving portions. Sprinkle with sesame seeds. Serve with a green salad and some fresh mango cut into thin slices.

GINGER SOY OYSTERS

PRAWNS WITH CREAMY COCONUT SAUCE

PRAWNS WITH CREAMY COCONUT SAUCE

Peel 24 large cooked king prawns, leaving the tails intact. Heat 1 tablespoon oil and 20 g butter in small pan. Add 1 clove crushed garlic, half a small finely chopped onion, 1–2 teaspoons mild or vindaloo curry paste, 1/2 teaspoon ground cumin, 1–2 teaspoons soft brown sugar and 2–3 tablespoons coconut cream. Cook over medium heat for 2–3 minutes or until mixture reduces and thickens slightly. Whisk through 1–2 tablespoons sour cream and 1 tablespoon finely chopped chives or coriander. Process until smooth. Place sauce in a bowl and serve warm or cool with peeled prawns for dipping.

SAVOURY BITES

NEW POTATOES WITH SPICY SOUR CREAM

SAVOURY BITES

Brush 4 sheets ready-rolled puff pastry with melted butter or oil. Place on four greased oven trays. Spread 2 sheets thinly with tomato paste and remaining 2 sheets with wholegrain mustard. Top tomato sheets with 2/3 cup quartered marinated artichoke hearts, 1/3 cup sliced black olives, 1–2 tablespoons fresh shredded basil and 1/3 cup grated mozzarella cheese. Sprinkle with crushed garlic, rock salt and freshly ground black pepper. Top mustard sheets with thin wedges of egg tomato, 3 slices salami cut in thin strips, and 125 g camembert cheese, thinly sliced. Sprinkle with cracked pepper. Bake in preheated moderately hot 210°C oven for 10–15 minutes, or until crisp. Cut into squares or triangles. Serve hot.

NEW POTATOES WITH SPICY SOUR CREAM

Steam or microwave 24 small new potatoes until just tender. Drain well; cool. Combine in a small bowl 2/3 cup sour cream, 3 teaspoons finely chopped chives or 2 teaspoons finely chopped lemon thyme, 2 teaspoons French or German mustard and 1 clove crushed garlic (optional). Mix well. Cut a small cross in the top of each potato and squeeze to open. Spoon a dollop of sour cream mixture on top of each potato. Top with red or black caviar, a small strip of anchovy fillet and a small sprig of thyme—or create your own toppings.

ORANGE GLAZED BARBECUED CHICKEN

Dips and Spreads

CHEESY NUT LOG

Place in food processor: 125 g chopped camembert cheese, $1/4$ cup grated cheddar cheese, 50 g softened cream cheese, 1 tablespoon chopped fresh chives, 3–4 teaspoons white wine or dry sherry, 1 clove crushed garlic (optional), salt and pepper to taste. Process 10–20 seconds only. Shape mixture into a log or flat round. Roll in finely crushed nuts. Serve with water crackers or savoury wafers.

MINTED CUCUMBER DIP

Finely grate 1 Lebanese cucumber; squeeze out excess moisture. Combine in bowl with 2 cloves crushed garlic, 1 cup plain yoghurt, 1 teaspoon each fresh chopped dill and mint, and salt and pepper. Mix well. Serve.

EGGPLANT DIP

Halve 2 small eggplants lengthways, sprinkle with salt; stand for 15–20 minutes. Rinse and pat dry with paper towel. Bake in moderate 180°C oven for 20 minutes or until soft. Peel away skin, discard. Place flesh in food processor with 3–4 cloves crushed garlic, 2 tablespoons lemon juice, 2 tablespoons tahini, 1 tablespoon olive oil, salt and pepper to taste. Process 20–30 seconds. Sprinkle paprika on top.

BEST-EVER GUACAMOLE

Combine in a medium bowl 1 large ripe mashed avocado, 2 tablespoons sour cream, 1 tablespoon mayonnaise, 4–5 teaspoons lemon juice, 1 small finely chopped red onion, 1 teaspoon each ground cumin and coriander, 1 clove crushed garlic, 1 finely chopped tomato, 1 tablespoon chopped chives, salt and pepper, and some chilli powder or Tabasco sauce to taste. Mix well to combine and serve with corn chips, crackers or crudités.

EGGPLANT DIP

CHEESY NUT LOG

MINTED CUCUMBER DIP

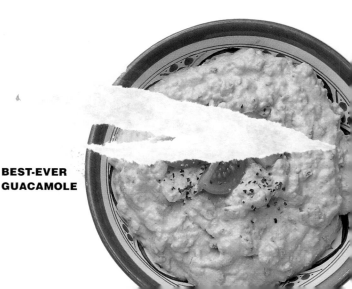

BEST-EVER GUACAMOLE

CREAMY HERB DIP

CREAMY HERB DIP

Beat 150 g cream cheese until light and creamy. Add 2 tablespoons each sour cream and whole egg mayonnaise, 2 tablespoons chopped chives, 1 tablespoon each chopped parsley, lemon thyme and basil, and salt and pepper to taste. Beat until smooth. Serve.

SMOKED TROUT PÂTÉ

Remove skin and bones from 2 small smoked trout. Place flesh in food processor, add 1/4 cup sour cream, 1/2 cup sieved cottage cheese, 1–2 tablespoons lemon juice, salt and pepper to taste. Process 20 seconds or until smooth. Spoon mixture into individual ramekin dishes. Cover and refrigerate overnight before serving.

HUMMUS

Place in food processor: one 425 g can drained garbanzos (chick peas), 2–3 tablespoons each lemon juice and olive oil, 2 cloves crushed garlic, and salt and pepper to taste. Process for 20–30 seconds or until smooth. Serve. Add 1/4 cup tahini paste to the mixture, if desired.

SMOKED TROUT PÂTÉ

HUMMUS

TOMATO AND OLIVE DIP

Heat 1 tablespoon olive oil and 20 g butter in a medium pan. Add 1 small finely chopped onion, 1 clove crushed garlic, 2 teaspoons Italian dried mixed herbs, 1 teaspoon cracked pepper and 1 teaspoon ground cumin. Cook over medium heat for 2 minutes. Stir in one 425 g can crushed tomatoes, 2 tablespoons tomato paste, 1/4 cup red wine and 1/2 cup tomato puree. Bring to boil, reduce heat; simmer 5–10 minutes or until sauce has thickened and reduced by half. Stir in 1/4 cup chopped black or green olives. Serve warm.

TOMATO AND OLIVE DIP

PARTY STARTERS

CHILLI PRAWN SKEWERS

Preparation time: 25 minutes
Total cooking time: 10 minutes
Makes 30

30 green king prawns
1/3 cup fresh coriander sprigs
2 tablespoons fresh basil leaves
50 g butter
1 clove garlic, crushed
2 teaspoons soft brown sugar
2 tablespoons lemon or lime juice
1 tablespoon sweet chilli sauce
pepper to taste

➤ REMOVE HEADS from prawns.
1 Peel prawns, leaving the tails intact. Using a sharp knife, slit each prawn down the back. Remove vein.
2 Finely chop coriander and basil.
3 Heat the butter in a large frying pan or wok. Add the garlic, sugar, juice, coriander, basil and sweet chilli sauce. Mix all together well. Toss the prawns through the mixture, then cook over medium heat for 4–5 minutes or until the prawns turn a pinkish colour and are cooked through. Sprinkle pepper over prawn mixture.

Thread prawns onto bamboo skewers or strong toothpicks. Serve warm.

COOK'S FILE

Storage time: Peel and devein the prawns several hours in advance. Cook them just before serving.
Variations: Prawns are also delicious grilled. Thread onto skewers and grill for 2–3 minutes. Brush the prawns with butter mixture during cooking. Scallops or oysters can be used instead of prawns, or alternate pieces of fish with prawns on skewer and add a few bay leaves (bay leaves are for flavouring only; they are too strong to eat). Try substituting herbs such as dill and parsley for the coriander and basil.
Hint: Raw prawn flesh is greyish in colour—the colour of the shell will vary between different species. The longer they stand, the darker they become. Look for prawns with pale flesh, a fresh salty smell and a firm shell; prawns which have been frozen often have a softer shell with spongy flesh. If using a barbecue to cook this dish (or any seafood), throw some herbs onto the coals. They will give off a delicious aroma during cooking and add a subtle flavour.

SWEET AND SALTY NUTS

Preparation time: 20 minutes
Total cooking time: 15 minutes
Serves 6–8

250 g blanched almonds
250 g pecans
1/4 cup sugar
1 teaspoon salt
1 teaspoon ground cinnamon
pinch ground cloves
1/2 teaspoon curry powder
1/4 teaspoon ground cumin
1/2 teaspoon ground black
    pepper

➤ PREHEAT OVEN to moderate 180°C.
1 Place almonds and pecans on a large baking tray. Bake 5–10 minutes or until golden and crisp. Remove nuts from oven, allow to cool.
2 Combine sugar, salt and spices in a small bowl. Mix well.
3 Heat a large frying pan. Add the almonds and pecans. Sprinkle the spice mixture over the nuts. Cook the nuts, stirring over medium heat for 5 minutes or until they turn golden. The sugar will melt and coat the nuts. Shake the frying pan often to ensure even cooking. If nuts stick together, separate them with a wooden spoon. When nuts are cooked, remove from heat. Spread them on a lightly oiled baking tray to cool.

COOK'S FILE

Storage time: Keep the cooled nuts in tightly sealed jars or containers. They will stay fresh for up to 12 days.
Hint: If using a small frying pan, cook the nuts in 2 smaller batches. Cashews, macadamias or peanuts can be substituted for almonds and pecans, or use a single variety.

1

2

3

HERB PEPPER CRISPS WITH BLUE CHEESE DIP

Preparation time: 20–25 minutes
Total cooking time: 5 minutes
Serves 10–15

4 sheets lavash bread
100 g butter, melted
1 small jar herb pepper
   seasoning
1 tablespoon finely chopped
   fresh chives

Blue Cheese Dip
250 g blue vein cheese, chopped
60 g butter, softened
1 tablespoon sweet white wine

2 teaspoons chopped fresh mint
1 teaspoon chopped fresh
   rosemary
2 teaspoons chopped fresh
   oregano
1/3 cup crème fraîche or sour
   cream
salt and pepper to taste

➤ PREHEAT OVEN to moderate 180°C.
1 Brush each sheet of lavash bread with butter. Sprinkle with herb pepper seasoning and chives.
2 Cut each sheet into 20 squares. Cut each piece in half to make triangles. Place triangles on baking trays. Bake 5 minutes or until crisp. Remove and cool. Serve with Blue Cheese Dip.

3 To make Blue Cheese Dip: Using electric beaters, beat cheese and butter in small mixing bowl until smooth and creamy. Add wine, mint, rosemary and oregano; mix well. Fold through crème fraîche or sour cream. Season with pepper and salt to taste. Spoon mixture into serving dishes.

COOK'S FILE

Storage time: Herb Pepper Crisps may be stored in an airtight container for up to 2 weeks.
Variation: Combine 2 cloves crushed garlic with melted butter before brushing over lavash bread. Sprinkle the bread with grated Parmesan cheese and chives, cut into squares and triangles, and bake.

CUCUMBER AND SALMON BITES

Preparation time: 20 minutes
Total cooking time: Nil
Makes about 40

4 medium Lebanese cucumbers
250 g cream cheese or
   neufchatel
210 g can red or pink salmon,
   drained
1 tablespoon sour cream
1 tablespoon mayonnaise
1–2 teaspoons lemon juice

1 tablespoon finely chopped
   coriander
1 tablespoon finely chopped
   chives
2 teaspoons finely chopped
   lemon thyme
salt and pepper, to taste

➤ WASH THE CUCUMBERS and trim ends.

1 Cut the cucumbers into slices 0.5 cm thick.

2 Beat the cream cheese in a small bowl using electric beaters until it is soft and creamy. Add the salmon, sour cream, mayonnaise, lemon juice, coriander, chives, lemon thyme, and salt and pepper. Beat 1 minute or until well combined.

3 Place a teaspoonful of the cheese mixture on the cucumber rounds. Decorate with sprigs of fresh dill.

COOK'S FILE

Storage time: The salmon mixture can be prepared a day ahead. Keep it in the refrigerator in an airtight container. Slice the cucumber into rounds and assemble just before serving.

Variation: Top the cheese mixture with thin shreds of fresh chilli or red capsicum to decorate.

PRUNE AND BACON SKEWERS

Preparation time: 35 minutes
Total cooking time: 5 minutes
Makes about 60

20 rashers bacon
125 g cream cheese
1 tablespoon mayonnaise
3 teaspoons German or French
   mustard
3 teaspoons finely chopped
   chives
2 x 375 g packets pitted prunes

➤ REMOVE RIND from bacon. Cut into 5 cm lengths.

1 Beat the cream cheese using electric beaters until soft and creamy. Add the mayonnaise, mustard and chives, and beat until all ingredients are thoroughly combined.

2 Using a piping bag, pipe the cream cheese mixture into the centre of each pitted prune.

3 Roll each prune in a strip of bacon and carefully secure the end of the bacon with a small bamboo skewer or toothpick. Grill under moderately hot grill for 3–5 minutes, turning frequently, until the bacon is crisp and browned. These can be served either hot from the grill or cold.

COOK'S FILE

Storage time: Prune and Bacon Skewers can be assembled up to a day in advance. Store in the refrigerator, covered, until needed. Cook skewers just before serving if serving hot. If serving as a cold hors d'oeuvre, cook beforehand, cool and refrigerate for several hours.

Hint: Soften cream cheese by bringing it to room temperature. Light cream cheese can be used if preferred.

CHEESE AND SPINACH ROULADE BRUSCHETTA

Preparation time: 30 minutes
Total cooking time: 10 minutes
Makes about 24

1 French bread stick
2 tablespoons oil
500 g English spinach
90 g cream cheese
90 g goats cheese
¼ cup finely chopped, canned pimiento, drained on sheet of paper towel

➤ PREHEAT OVEN to moderately hot 200°C (gas 190°C).

1 Cut bread into thin slices. Brush slices lightly on each side with oil. Place in single layer on an oven tray. Bake for 10 minutes or until lightly browned, turning once.

2 Remove stalks from spinach leaves, place leaves into a bowl. Cover with boiling water, stand for about 3 minutes or until leaves have softened. Drain and cool. Squeeze out excess liquid; drain on sheets of paper towel.

3 Lay spinach leaves flat, overlapping each other on a piece of plastic wrap, to form a 25 x 20 cm rectangle. Beat cheeses together until smooth.

Spread cheese mixture evenly over the spinach. Top cheese evenly with pimento. Using the plastic wrap as a guide, carefully roll up spinach to enclose the cheese. Remove plastic wrap and cut log into thin slices. Serve on the slices of baked bread.

COOK'S FILE

Storage time: Bread slices can be baked several days ahead. Store in an airtight container. The roulade can be made a day ahead. Store, wrapped in plastic wrap, in the refrigerator. Assemble just before serving.

Hint: Be sure to drain spinach and pimento well to avoid a watery result.

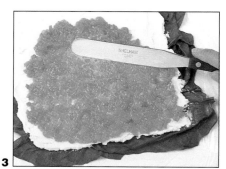

SMOKED SALMON BLINI

Preparation time: 15 minutes
Total cooking time: 10–15 minutes
Makes about 50

Blini
1 cup self-raising flour
2 eggs, lightly beaten
1/2 cup milk
1 tablespoon sour cream

Topping
1/2 cup sour cream
2 tablespoons mayonnaise
2 teaspoons lemon juice

1 tablespoon finely chopped
   chives
1 tablespoon finely chopped
   mint
125 g sliced smoked salmon

➤ SIFT FLOUR in mixing bowl, make a well in the centre.
1 Add combined eggs, milk and cream; stir until batter is smooth and free of lumps. Let stand 10 minutes.
2 Heat a large non-stick frying pan, brush with oil or melted butter. Drop teaspoonsful of mixture into pan. When bubbles appear on surface, turn blinis, cook other side. Remove and set aside. Repeat with rest of mixture.

3 Combine the sour cream, mayonnaise, lemon juice, chives and mint. Spoon a small amount of sour cream mixture on top of each blini. Top with a slice of smoked salmon and decorate with strips of lemon peel.

COOK'S FILE:

Storage time: Sour cream mixture can be made a day ahead. Assemble up to 1 hour ahead.
Variation: Substitute smoked trout for the salmon. Top with finely chopped capers. Replace the blinis with thin slices of French bread stick. Top with the sour cream mixture and smoked fish, and serve.

SUSHI ROLLS

Preparation time: 45 minutes
Total cooking time: 5–10 minutes
Makes about 30

1 cup short grain white rice
2 cups water
2 tablespoons rice vinegar
1 tablespoon sugar
1 teaspoon salt
3–4 sheets of Nori (see note)
wasabi to taste, optional (see note)
125 g smoked salmon, trout or
    fresh sashimi tuna
1 small Lebanese cucumber,
    peeled
1/2 small avocado
1/4 cup pickled ginger
soy sauce for dipping

➤ WASH RICE in cold water, drain well. Place rice and water in medium pan.

Bring to boil, reduce heat and simmer uncovered for 4–5 minutes or until all the water is absorbed. Cover, reduce heat to very low and cook for another 4–5 minutes. Remove pan from heat and cool.

1 Stir combined vinegar, sugar and salt into rice. Place 1 sheet of Nori onto a piece of greaseproof paper on a flat work surface.

2 Place a quarter of the rice along one end of the Nori, leaving a 2 cm border around the three sides. Spread a very small amount of wasabi down centre of the rice.

3 Cut the fish into thin strips, and the cucumber and the avocado into small pieces.

4 Place the pieces of fish, cucumber, avocado and ginger over the wasabi.

5 Using the paper as a guide, roll up firmly from the bottom, enclosing in the rice the ingredients placed in the centre. Press Nori to seal edges.

6 Using a sharp flat-bladed or electric knife, cut roll into 2.5 cm rounds. Repeat the process with remaining ingredients. Serve sushi rolls with small shallow bowls of soy sauce, or extra wasabi mixed with soy sauce, for dipping.

Storage time: Sushi rolls can be made several hours in advance. Store them covered in the refrigerator and slice just before serving.

Note: Nori is an edible seaweed which is sold pressed into dried sheets. Wasabi is similar to horseradish cream but is a pale green colour. As the flavour is much hotter than horseradish, use it very sparingly, adjusting quantities according to personal taste. Wasabi is available as a paste or in powdered form from most Asian food stores, and many health food shops also stock ingredients for Asian dishes. Sashimi tuna is available from good fishmongers or fish markets. Make sure that it is extremely fresh. Frozen fish is not suitable for use in this dish.

CRAB DIP WITH SPICY SAUCE AND CRUDITÉS

Preparation time: 30 minutes
Total cooking time: Nil
Serves 10

2 x 200 g cans crab meat, drained
500 g cream cheese, softened
1/3 cup mayonnaise
1/3 cup fresh chopped chives
2 tablespoons fresh chopped chives, extra

Spicy Sauce
2 tablespoons Father's Favourite sauce
2 tablespoons tomato sauce

2 tablespoons spicy barbecue sauce
1–2 teaspoons worcestershire sauce
vegetables for crudités: carrot and celery sticks, broccoli florets, capsicum strips, button mushrooms

➤ PREPARE vegetables for crudités.

1 Place three quarters of the crab meat in mixing bowl. Add cream cheese, mayonnaise and chives. Beat with electric beaters until smooth.

2 Spoon mixture into serving bowl, sprinkle with remaining crab and extra chives. Cover and refrigerate.

3 **To make Spicy Sauce:** Combine sauces in small bowl, mix well. Transfer mixture to a serving jug.

To serve: Pour a small amount of sauce to cover the surface of the dip. Serve with crudités. Pour more sauce over the dip as needed.

COOK'S FILE

Storage time: Both Dip and Spicy Sauce can be made a day in advance. Cover and store in the refrigerator.

Hint: Fresh crab meat can be used instead of canned. The best value cooked crabs are those that are heavy for their size, indicating they have grown to fill their latest shell. Choose crabs with dry, bright shells with no cracks or holes and a fresh, pleasant smell. A bleached appearance is normal. Crab sizes vary greatly but the larger they are the easier it is to extract the meat.

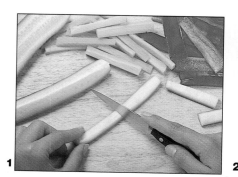

1

2

3

SPICY TORTILLA TRIANGLES

Preparation time: 20 minutes
Total cooking time: 5 minutes
Makes 24

2 x 23 cm flour tortillas
1/4 cup oil, approximately

Topping
1 tablespoon oil
1 onion, finely chopped
2 cloves garlic, crushed
2 small red chillies, finely chopped
425 g can pinto beans, drained, mashed roughly
1 cup bottled thick and chunky salsa

2 tablespoons chopped coriander
2/3 cup grated cheddar cheese

➤ CUT TORTILLAS into quarters. Cut each quarter into 3 triangles.
1 Heat 2 tablespoons of the oil in a frying pan. Add a few triangles to pan, cook for 30 seconds on each side or until crisp and golden brown. Remove from pan, drain on paper towel. Repeat with the remaining triangles, adding extra oil as necessary.
2 To make Topping: Heat oil in a medium pan, add onion, garlic and chilli, stir over medium heat for 3 minutes or until onion is tender. Stir in beans, salsa and coriander. Remove from heat and cool.
3 Spread topping on triangles and

sprinkle with cheese. Cook under pre-heated grill for 1 minute or until the cheese has melted.

COOK'S FILE

Storage time: Tortilla triangles can be made a day ahead; store in an air-tight container. Topping can be made a day ahead and stored in the refrigerator. Assemble triangles up to 1 hour ahead. Grill just before serving.
Hint: Tortillas and bottled salsa are available from supermarkets and delicatessens. Tortilla triangles can be cooked in the oven instead of fried or grilled. Place triangles on a baking tray in a preheated moderate 180°C oven for 5 minutes or until crisp. Add topping, cook for another 3–5 minutes or until the cheese has melted.

CHEESE, BASIL AND PINE NUT TRIANGLES

Preparation time: 30 minutes
Total cooking time: 15 minutes
Makes 28

125 g feta cheese
125 g ricotta cheese
2 tablespoons chopped
    fresh basil
1/4 cup pine nuts, toasted
1 egg, lightly beaten
salt and pepper to taste
14 sheets filo pastry
125 g butter, melted

➤ PREHEAT OVEN to moderately hot 200°C (gas 190°C).

1 Combine the cheeses, basil, pine nuts and egg in a medium bowl. Season with salt and pepper to taste.

2 Place a sheet of pastry on a work surface and brush all over with melted butter. Top with another sheet of pastry, brush with butter. Cut the pastry lengthways into four strips.

3 Place 3 level teaspoons of the mixture on the end of each strip. Fold pastry over and up to enclose filling and form a triangle. Brush triangles with butter, place on an oven tray. Repeat the process with the remaining pastry and filling. Bake triangles for 15 minutes or until golden brown. Serve hot.

COOK'S FILE

Storage time: Triangles can be assembled several hours ahead; cook just before serving. Cooked triangles can be frozen in a single layer on an oven tray until firm, then transferred to an airtight container.

Hint: Handle filo pastry quickly and carefully as it becomes brittle when exposed to air. Cover spare sheets with a damp tea-towel while assembling triangles.

Variation: Grill 4 lean bacon rashers until crisp. Crumble and add to filling.

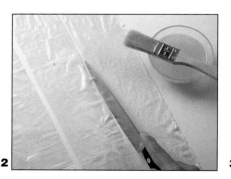

CRAB CAKES WITH AVOCADO DIP

Preparation time: 30 minutes
Total cooking time: 4 minutes per
  batch
Makes about 30

500 g crab meat
2 cups fresh breadcrumbs
1/2 cup mayonnaise
4 spring onions, chopped
1/4 cup chopped fresh coriander
2 tablespoons lemon juice
1 teaspoon grated lemon rind
1 teaspoon sambal oelek
2 eggs, lightly beaten
oil for shallow frying

Avocado Dip
1 small, ripe avocado
1 clove garlic, crushed
1/3 cup plain yoghurt
1/4 cup water

➤ PREHEAT OVEN to moderate
180°C.
1 Combine crab meat, breadcrumbs,
mayonnaise, spring onions, coriander,
lemon juice, sambal oelek and eggs
in a large bowl.
2 Heat 1 tablespoon of oil in frying
pan. Drop tablespoonsful of mixture,
about 2 cm apart, into pan. Cook crab
cakes over medium heat for 2 minutes
or until undersides are golden. Turn
and cook for 2 minutes more. Remove
from pan and drain on paper towel.
Keep cakes warm in oven. Repeat
with remaining mixture, adding more
oil to pan as needed to prevent sticking. Serve with Avocado Dip.
3 To make Avocado Dip: Place
avocado, garlic, yoghurt and water in
food processor bowl or blender. Using
pulse action, process for 10 seconds or
until mixture is smooth and creamy.

COOK'S FILE

Storage time: Crab mixture can be
made a day ahead. Cook just before
serving. Dip can be made several
hours in advance and covered.
Variation: Canned crab meat can be
used for this recipe if preferred.
Canned tuna or salmon could also be
used, if desired. For an economical
alternative, substitute other firm
fleshed white fish, cooked and flaked;
or chop raw fish very finely.

SWEET CHILLI WINGS

Preparation time: 30 minutes
+ refrigeration
Total cooking time: 1 hour 30 minutes–
1 hour 45 minutes
Serves 10

2 kg chicken wings
2 cloves garlic, crushed
1/4 teaspoon salt
1 teaspoon ground black pepper
1 tablespoon oil
1/4 cup sweet chilli sauce
2 tablespoons honey
1 tablespoon white vinegar
1/4 cup soy sauce
2 teaspoons grated ginger
1 tablespoon soft brown sugar

➤ PREHEAT OVEN to moderate 180°C.

1 Trim chicken of excess fat and sinew. Cut each wing into 3 sections, discard tips (freeze them and use for making stock).

2 Combine the remaining ingredients in a large mixing bowl. Mix well. Add the chicken pieces and stir until coated. Cover and refrigerate several hours or overnight.

3 Drain the chicken pieces and reserve marinade. Place chicken pieces on a roasting rack over an oven tray or place them in a deep baking dish. Bake for 1 1/2 hours or until chicken is crisp and cooked through. Brush the pieces with reserved marinade several times during cooking. Serve hot.

COOK'S FILE

Storage time: Cook chicken up to 2 days in advance. Store, covered, in the refrigerator. Reheat in a moderate oven for 10–15 minutes or until hot.

Variation: Add fresh chopped chives and coriander to the marinade.

1

2

3

PARMESAN AND PESTO TOASTS

Preparation time: 15 minutes
Total cooking time: 5 minutes
Makes about 40

3 small torpedo or hot dog rolls
16 large sun-dried tomatoes, cut into thin strips
150 g fresh parmesan cheese, shaved thinly

Pesto
1 cup packed basil leaves
2 tablespoons fresh chopped chives
1/3 cup pine nuts
2–3 cloves garlic, peeled
1/4 cup olive oil

➤ FREEZE ROLLS until firm.
1 Cut frozen rolls into very thin slices using a serrated knife. Toast bread slices under a hot grill until they are golden brown on both sides.

2 To make Pesto: Place the basil leaves, chives, pine nuts, garlic and olive oil in a food processor. Process for 20–30 seconds or until smooth.
3 Spread pesto mixture evenly over toasted slices. Top with strips of tomato and shavings of cheese.

COOK'S FILE

Storage time: Bread slices can be toasted up to one week in advance. Store in an airtight container. Assemble just before serving.

SMALL FINGER SANDWICHES

Preparation time: 30 minutes
Total cooking time: Nil
Makes 84

125 g camembert cheese, chopped
80 g cream cheese or butter, softened
2 teaspoons finely chopped dill or lemon thyme
1 loaf white sliced bread
1 loaf brown sliced bread
100 g smoked salmon slices
1 medium avocado, mashed
2 teaspoons lemon juice
salt and pepper to taste
100 g sliced leg ham or pastrami

➤ PLACE CAMEMBERT, cream cheese and dill or lemon thyme in a small mixing bowl.

1 Using electric beaters, beat mixture until smooth and well combined. Spread 7 slices of bread with the cheese mixture.

2 Top each slice of bread with a slice of smoked salmon and then another slice of bread. Combine avocado, lemon juice, salt and pepper.

3 Spread a thin layer of the avocado mixture over each slice of bread. Top with a third slice of bread. Press sandwiches firmly together. Set aside. Repeat the layering process with another 7 slices of bread, substituting slices of leg ham or slices of pastrami for the smoked salmon. Wrap each sandwich in plastic wrap (there will be 14 whole sandwiches). Refrigerate for at least 1 hour.

4 To serve: Cut the crusts from the sandwiches, using an electric or serrated knife. Cut the sandwiches in half vertically and then across into 3 fingers. Each sandwich will make 6 small fingers. See variations below.

COOK'S FILE

Storage time: Sandwiches can be made several hours in advance. Store, covered, in the refrigerator. Cut into fingers just before serving.

Hint: Sandwiches can be kept fresh before guests arrive if they are covered on their serving dish with a clean, damp tea-towel.

Variation: Make triangle sandwiches by cutting each whole sandwich into 4 squares, then cutting each square into a triangle. Use alternating layers of brown and white breads. Cut into a variety of shapes and sizes with decorative biscuit cutters. Alternative fillings could include slices of turkey breast or smoked chicken.

BACON AND ONION QUICHES

Preparation time: 40 minutes
  + 30 minutes refrigeration
Total cooking time: 40 minutes
Makes 24

oil or melted butter
2 cups plain flour
150 g butter, chopped
3–4 tablespoons milk
plain flour, extra

Filling
3 rashers bacon, rind removed
2 teaspoons oil
1 onion, thinly sliced
salt and pepper, to taste
¼ teaspoon mustard powder
1 cup milk
2 eggs, lightly beaten
⅓ cup cream
2 tablespoons finely chopped
    chives
⅓ cup grated cheddar cheese

➤ BRUSH TWO 12-cup deep patty tins with melted butter or oil.

1 Place flour and butter in a food processor bowl. Process for 10–15 seconds or until mixture is fine and crumbly. Add milk, process a further 10–15 seconds or until mixture just comes together. Turn out onto a lightly floured surface. Knead dough lightly until smooth.

2 Roll out pastry to 2 mm thickness. Using an 8 cm cutter, cut pastry into rounds. Ease pastry rounds into prepared tins. Refrigerate 30 minutes.

3 To make Filling: Preheat oven to moderate 180°C. Chop bacon. Heat oil in frying pan; add onion, bacon, salt, pepper and mustard. Cook over medium heat for 3–5 minutes or until onion is golden and bacon slightly crisp. Cool slightly.

4 Combine milk, eggs, cream and chives; mix well. Divide the bacon mixture evenly between the pastry cases. Pour the egg mixture on top and sprinkle with cheese. Bake for 15 minutes or until golden. Stand the quiches in their tins for 5 minutes. Remove and serve warm.

COOK'S FILE

Storage time: Pastry shells can be prepared up to 4 hours ahead. Assemble the filling and bake the quiches just before serving.
Hint: If preferred, fresh smoked salmon may be used in place of the bacon. Add the salmon to the egg mixture in step 3.

BOCCONCINI TOMATO SKEWERS

Preparation time: 20 minutes
+ refrigeration
Total cooking time: Nil
Makes 20

20 very small whole bocconcini
or 5 larger ones sliced into
quarters
1 tablespoon fresh parsley
2 teaspoons chopped fresh
chives
2 tablespoons olive oil
1/4 teaspoon salt
1/2 teaspoon ground black
pepper
20 small cherry tomatoes
40 small fresh basil leaves

➤ PLACE BOCCONCINI in a bowl.
1 Finely chop the parsley.
2 Add oil, parsley, chives, salt and pepper to the bocconcini. Cover and refrigerate for at least 1 hour, or preferably overnight.
3 Cut each cherry tomato in half. Place one half on a skewer or tooth-pick. Thread on a basil leaf, then bocconcini, another basil leaf and then another tomato half. Do the same with more skewers and the remaining ingredients and serve.

COOK'S FILE

Storage time: Skewers can be served immediately, or covered and chilled for up to 8 hours.
Hint: Bocconcini are small moulded patties of fresh mozzarella cheese used in antipasto and salads. They are available from most delicatessens and larger supermarkets.

MUSTARD EGGS

Preparation time: 40 minutes
Total cooking time: 10 minutes
Makes 40

20 x 55 g eggs
1 tablespoon mayonnaise
1 tablespoon sour cream
2–3 teaspoons Dijon mustard
1 tablespoon very finely
    chopped parsley or finely
    chopped chives
1 tablespoon finely chopped
    chives, extra

➤ PLACE EGGS in large heavy-based pan, cover with water.

1 Stir eggs gently over low heat until water boils. Cook for 10 minutes. Remove from heat, cool.

2 Cut the eggs in half, carefully remove the yolks. Place the yolks, mayonnaise, sour cream, mustard and parsley or chives in a medium bowl. Stir until the mixture becomes smooth and creamy.

3 Place the egg yolk mixture into a piping bag fitted with a fluted nozzle. Pipe stars of yolk mixture into the egg white cavities. Decorate Mustard Eggs with chives and serve.

COOK'S FILE

Storage time: Eggs can be boiled several hours in advance. Pipe the yolk mixture into the cavities and decorate just prior to serving.
Variation: Flavour the yolk mixture with curry powder or powdered mustard in place of the Dijon mustard. Top with red and black caviar to decorate instead of chives.
Hint: Eggs should be at room temperature before being boiled to reduce the possibility of cracking. A couple of tablespoons of vinegar in the water may help to seal any leaks from small cracks if they do occur.

ROSEMARY AND CHEESE BISCUITS

Preparation time: 10 minutes
    +15 minutes refrigeration
Total cooking time: 20 minutes
Makes 50

oil or melted butter
1 cup plain flour
100 g chilled butter, chopped
1 tablespoon sour cream
60 g cheddar cheese, grated
60 g shredded parmesan
    cheese
1/4 teaspoon salt

3 teaspoons chopped fresh
    rosemary
3 teaspoons chopped fresh
    chives
1/2 teaspoon black pepper

➤ PREHEAT OVEN to moderate 180°C. Brush two oven trays with melted butter or oil.

1 Sift the flour into a medium mixing bowl. Using fingertips, rub the butter into the flour until the mixture is fine and crumbly.

2 Add sour cream, cheeses, salt, herbs and pepper; mix well with a knife. Press mixture together until it forms a soft dough. Wrap in plastic wrap; refrigerate for 10–15 minutes.

3 Roll level teaspoons of mixture into balls. Place onto prepared trays, allowing space for spreading. Flatten balls with a floured fork. Bake 15–20 minutes or until lightly golden. Transfer biscuits to wire rack to cool.

COOK'S FILE

Storage time: Make biscuits up to 1 week in advance; store in airtight container. Alternatively, prepare dough up to 2 days in advance and refrigerate until ready to use.
Hint: Omit salt from the recipe. Sprinkle uncooked biscuits with crushed sea salt or rock salt.

*Opposite: Mustard Eggs (top),
Rosemary and Cheese Biscuits (bottom).*

OLIVE AND ROSEMARY PALMIERS

Preparation time: 20 minutes
Total cooking time: 15 minutes
Makes 30

oil or melted butter
1/2 cup chopped, pitted black
    olives
1/3 cup grated parmesan cheese
1 tablespoon chopped rosemary
4 slices salami, chopped
2 tablespoons oil
2 teaspoons Dijon mustard
2 sheets ready-rolled puff pastry

➤ PREHEAT OVEN to moderately
hot 200°C (gas 190°C). Brush two oven
trays with melted butter or oil.
1 Combine olives, cheese, rosemary,
salami, oil and mustard in a blender or
food processor. Process for 30 seconds
or until mixture becomes a paste.
2 Place a sheet of pastry on work surface and spread evenly with half the
olive paste. Fold two opposite sides
over to meet edge to edge in the centre. Fold once again, then fold in half
to give 8 layers of pastry.
3 Cut into 1 cm slices. Lay slices, cut
side up, on prepared trays; allow room
for spreading. Open slices out slightly
at the folded end to give a V shape.
Repeat with remaining pastry and
olive paste. Bake for 15 minutes or
until golden brown.

COOK'S FILE

Storage time: Palmiers can be prepared in advance, covered and refrigerated. Bake just before serving, or
bake and reheat in a moderate oven
(180°C) 5 minutes. Palmiers can also
be frozen, cooked or not. Place on oven
trays in a single layer, freeze until
firm then transfer to freezer container.

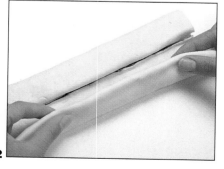

WONTON WITH HONEY CHILLI DIP

Preparation time: 40 minutes
Total cooking time: 10–15 minutes
Makes 48

250 g lean pork
100 g green prawns, peeled
60 g bamboo shoots, drained
3 spring onions, chopped
1 cm piece fresh ginger, peeled
salt and white pepper
1/4 cup chopped unsalted peanuts
1/2 teaspoon sugar
1 tablespoon chopped coriander
48 round egg pastry wonton
    wrappers
oil for deep frying

Honey Chilli Dip
1/4 cup honey
1/4 cup sweet chilli sauce
1 teaspoon chopped fresh ginger
1 teaspoon rice vinegar

➤ TRIM PORK of excess fat and sinew. Cut into cubes.

1 Place pork, prawns, bamboo shoots, onions and ginger in food processor. Process for 20–30 seconds or until mixture is smooth.

2 Transfer mixture to a medium bowl. Add salt, pepper, peanuts, sugar and coriander; mix well. Place 1 teaspoon of mixture into the centre of each wrapper. Brush edges with a little water. Bring the wrapper edges together to form pouches and squeeze gently to secure.

3 Heat oil in a deep, heavy-based pan. Lower wonton pouches into moderately hot oil. Cook in batches over medium heat for 1 minute or until golden, crisp and cooked through. Remove from oil with a slotted spoon; drain on paper towels. Serve wontons hot with Honey Chilli Dip.

To make Honey Chilli Dip: Combine honey, sweet chilli sauce, ginger and rice vinegar in a small bowl; mix well.

COOK'S FILE

Storage time: Make the wontons up to two days ahead. Store, covered, in refrigerator. Reheat in a moderate oven for 5–10 minutes or until crisp. Honey Chilli Dip can be made up to a week in advance.

HERB MEATBALLS WITH RICH TOMATO SAUCE

Preparation time: 40 minutes
Total cooking time: 10–15 minutes
Makes about 45

1 medium onion, finely chopped
750 g beef mince
1 egg, lightly beaten
2 cloves garlic, crushed
2 teaspoons cracked black pepper
1/4 teaspoon salt
2 tablespoons plum sauce
1 tablespoon worcestershire sauce
2 tablespoons finely chopped
    rosemary
1–2 tablespoons finely chopped
    mint or sweet basil
oil for frying

Rich Tomato Sauce
1 1/2 cups red wine
1 clove garlic, crushed
3/4 cup tomato purée
1/3 cup chunky bottled tomato
    sauce
2–3 teaspoons Dijon mustard
30 g butter, cut into pieces

➤ COMBINE ONION, beef, egg, garlic, pepper, salt, sauces and herbs in a large mixing bowl.

1 Use hands to combine well. Shape level tablespoons of mixture into balls.

2 Heat oil in a large frying pan. Cook meatballs in batches over medium heat for 5 minutes or until evenly browned. Shake the pan during cooking to prevent sticking. Drain on paper towel. Keep warm.

3 To make Tomato Sauce: Drain oil from pan, add wine and garlic to pan juices. Bring to boil, reduce heat, simmer to reduce liquid by half. Strain into medium pan. Add tomato purée, sauce and mustard. Bring to boil,

reduce heat and reduce liquid by half. Gradually whisk in butter. Serve warm.

COOK'S FILE

Storage time: Meatballs can be prepared up to 2 weeks in advance. Store them in the freezer in an airtight container. Thaw and reheat in moderate (180°C) oven for 10–15 minutes, or freeze raw and cook just before serving. The sauce can be made a day ahead. Reheat gently to serve.

1

2

3

PRAWN TOASTS

Preparation time: 20 minutes
Total cooking time: 10–15 minutes
Makes 48

350 g green prawns
1 clove garlic
75 g canned water chestnuts or
bamboo shoots, drained
1 tablespoon chopped fresh
coriander
2 cm piece ginger, peeled
2 eggs, separated
1/4 teaspoon white pepper
1/4 teaspoon salt
12 slices white bread

1 cup sesame seeds
oil for deep frying

➤ PEEL AND devein the prawns; discard tails.

1 Place prawn meat, garlic, chestnuts or bamboo shoots, coriander, ginger, egg white, pepper and salt in a food processor bowl. Process for 20–30 seconds or until mixture is smooth. Using a 5 cm round cutter, cut rounds from the bread slices.

2 Brush top of each bread round with lightly beaten egg yolk, then spread each evenly with the prawn mixture. Sprinkle with sesame seeds.

3 Heat oil in a deep heavy-based pan until moderately hot. Deep-fry the toasts in small batches, with the prawn mixture face down, for 10–15 seconds or until they are golden and crisp. Ensure that both sides are cooked. Remove toasts from the oil with tongs or with a slotted spoon. Drain them well on sheets of paper towel. Serve hot with chilli or sweet and sour sauce.

COOK'S FILE

Storage time: Prawn toasts can be prepared several hours ahead. Store, assembled and covered, in the refrigerator; deep-fry just before serving.
Hint: Use lemon juice to remove fishy smell from the skin after prawns have been handled.

MINI SPRING ROLLS

Preparation time: 40 minutes
Total cooking time: 3 minutes per
 batch
Makes 48

30 g bean thread vermicelli or
 rice stick noodles
150 g pork mince
1 medium carrot, grated
60 g bamboo shoots, drained,
 finely chopped
1 medium onion,
 finely chopped
2 spring onions,
 finely chopped
1/4 teaspoon salt
1/4 teaspoon black pepper

3 teaspoons fish sauce
12 large spring roll wrappers
peanut oil, for deep frying

➤ PLACE NOODLES in medium
bowl. Cover with boiling water. Stand
3 minutes, drain and set aside.
1 With scissors, cut the noodles into
small pieces.
2 Combine noodles, mince, carrot,
bamboo shoots, onions, salt, pepper
and sauce in a medium bowl. Mix
until well combined. Cut each spring
roll wrapper into four squares. Work
with two wrappers at a time, keeping
the remaining wrappers covered with
a clean, damp tea-towel to prevent
drying out. Place one heaped teaspoon
of mixture on each spring roll wrapper. Fold one corner over, then sides.

3 Roll up and seal with a little combined flour and water. Continue
process with the remaining mixture
and wrappers. Heat oil in a deep
heavy-based pan or wok until moderately hot. Carefully lower 3–4 spring
rolls into the oil using tongs or a slotted spoon. Cook for 3 minutes or until
wontons are golden and crisp. Drain
on paper towel. Serve hot with sweet
chilli or soy sauce.

COOK'S FILE

Storage time: Make spring rolls
several hours ahead. Cover and refrigerate. Deep-fry just before serving, or
reheat cooked spring rolls in a moderate 180°C oven for 10–15 minutes.
Variation: Use beef or chicken mince
in place of pork mince.

CAPSICUM ROLLS

Preparation time: 30 minutes
+12 hours refrigeration
Total cooking time: 12 minutes
Makes 20

1 large red capsicum
1/2 cup grated cheddar cheese
1/3 cup shredded parmesan
   cheese
2 tablespoons whole egg
   mayonnaise
2 tablespoons finely chopped
   parsley
1 teaspoon chopped fresh thyme
1 teaspoon chopped fresh oregano
salt and pepper to taste
2–3 drops Tabasco sauce
10 slices fresh bread
45 g butter, melted
paprika

➤ HALVE CAPSICUM and remove seeds and membrane. Brush skin with a little oil.

1 Grill capsicum, cut side down, until the skin is black. Cover with damp tea-towel until cool. Peel and discard skin. Finely chop the flesh and combine in a medium mixing bowl with cheeses, mayonnaise, herbs, salt, pepper and Tabasco. Cut crusts from bread, flatten slices with rolling pin. Brush both sides of slices with melted butter.

2 Spread capsicum mixture on each slice, leaving a 1 cm border. Roll up and secure with toothpick. Cover and refrigerate for up to 12 hours.

3 Cut each roll in half. Ensure a toothpick secures each roll. Place on oven tray. Bake in a preheated moderate 180°C oven for 10–12 minutes or until rolls are crisp and have turned a pale golden colour. Sprinkle with paprika. Serve warm.

COOK'S FILE

Storage time: Capsicum rolls can be prepared up to a day in advance. Bake just before serving.

Variation: Rolls can be served like mini rolled pizzas with different fillings. Brush bread slices with oil, then spread with tomato-paste. Sprinkle with sliced olives, sundried tomatoes, parmesan cheese, and chopped anchovies, mushrooms or other favourite fillings.

Note: These rolls, with simple but tasty fillings, make ideal children's party fare and can be easy enough for children to make themselves.

1

2

3

MUSHROOMS EN CROÛTE

Preparation time: 40 minutes
Total cooking time: 20 minutes
Makes 48

8 slices white bread
80 g butter, melted
1 tablespoon olive oil
1 clove garlic, crushed
½ small onion, finely chopped
375 g small button mushrooms, finely sliced
salt and pepper to taste
1 tablespoon dry sherry
2 teaspoons cornflour
⅓ cup sour cream
1 tablespoon finely chopped parsley
1 teaspoon finely chopped fresh thyme
¼ cup shredded parmesan cheese

➤ PREHEAT OVEN to moderate 180°C.

1 Cut the crusts from the bread. Brush both sides of bread with the melted butter. Cut each slice in half vertically, then each half into three horizontally. Place bread croûtes onto a foil-lined tray. Bake 5–10 minutes or until golden and crisp.

2 Heat the oil in a large frying pan; add the garlic and onion. Cook, stirring over low heat, until onion is soft. Add the mushrooms and cook over medium heat for 5 minutes or until tender. Season with salt and pepper.

3 Pour in the sherry. Blend the cornflour and sour cream, add to mushroom mixture and stir until mixture boils and thickens. Remove pan from heat and stir in the parsley and thyme. Set aside to cool.

4 Spread the mushroom mixture onto each croûte. Top with parmesan cheese. Place on a baking tray and bake for 5 minutes or until croûtes are heated through. Serve decorated with basil, if desired.

COOK'S FILE

Storage time: Make bread croûtes up to 4 days in advance and store in an airtight container. Make the mushroom topping and assemble just prior to serving.

Variation: Purée the mushroom mixture and spoon into small dishes; chill. Serve as a pâté with the bread croûtes.

Hint: If mushrooms need to be cleaned, they should be wiped with a damp cloth. Washing them dilutes the flavour as they absorb water easily. Store fresh mushrooms in a paper bag in the refrigerator before use. A plastic bag or container will cause them to sweat and deteriorate quickly.

CHICKEN SATAY WITH PEANUT SAUCE

Preparation time: 40 minutes
 + refrigeration
Total cooking time: 10 minutes
Makes 30

750 g chicken tenderloins or
 breast fillet
1 tablespoon fish sauce
2 teaspoons ground coriander
2 tablespoons fresh chopped
 coriander roots and stems
1 teaspoon black pepper
2 cloves garlic, crushed

Peanut Sauce
1 tablespoon peanut oil
1 medium onion, finely chopped

2–3 cloves garlic, crushed
1 teaspoon ground cumin
1/2 teaspoon ground coriander
1/2 teaspoon turmeric
1/2 cup crunchy peanut butter
1 tablespoon sweet chilli sauce
3/4 cup coconut cream

➤ TRIM CHICKEN of excess fat and sinew. If using breast fillets, cut into thin diagonal strips.

1 Thread chicken onto skewers. Place side by side in a flat non-metal dish. Combine sauce, coriander, pepper and garlic. Spread over chicken skewers. Cover with plastic wrap. Refrigerate 2 hours or overnight.

2 To make Peanut Sauce: Heat oil in a medium pan. Add the onion and cook over medium heat for 2 minutes. Add garlic, cumin, coriander and

turmeric, and cook, stirring, for 1 minute. Stir in the peanut butter, chilli sauce and coconut cream, mixing well. Stir over low heat until completely heated through.

3 Place chicken skewers on a lightly oiled barbecue grill or flat plate, or under a preheated grill, for 3–5 minutes, turning once. Grill until browned and cooked through. Serve warm with Peanut Sauce.

COOK'S FILE

Storage time: Chicken skewers can be prepared a day ahead. Cook just before serving. Make sauce several hours ahead; reheat gently, and add a little water if sauce is too thick.

Hint: To prevent bamboo skewers burning, soak in cold water for 20 minutes before threading on chicken.

GRAND MARNIER PÂTÉ

Preparation time: 30 minutes
  + refrigeration
Total cooking time: 10–15 minutes
Serves 8

125 g butter
500 g chicken livers or duck
  livers
1 medium onion, chopped
2 spring onions, chopped
2 cloves garlic, crushed
2–3 tablespoons Grand Marnier
1/2 cup cream
2 teaspoons chopped fresh thyme

2 teaspoons chopped fresh
  parsley or chives
salt and pepper
12 slices white or brown bread

➤TRIM LIVERS of sinew. Heat butter in large heavy-based frying pan.
1 Place livers, onions, garlic and Grand Marnier in frying pan. Stir over medium heat until the liver is just cooked and onion is soft. Bring to boil and simmer 4–5 minutes. Remove from heat, cool slightly.
2 Place mixture in a food processor bowl. Process for 20–30 seconds or until smooth. Add cream; process for 10 seconds. Transfer mixture to a

medium bowl. Stir in herbs. Season with salt and pepper, mix well. Spoon into small ramekins, or one large ramekin dish. Refrigerate overnight or until firm. Serve with Melba Toasts.
3 To make Melba Toasts: Cut crusts from bread. Flatten slices with a rolling pin; cut each in half, or quarter diagonally. Bake in a preheated moderate 180°C oven 5–10 minutes or until crisp and lightly golden. Cool.

COOK'S FILE

Storage: Make Pâté up to three days in advance. Cover and refrigerate. Melba Toasts can be made a week ahead. Store in an airtight container.

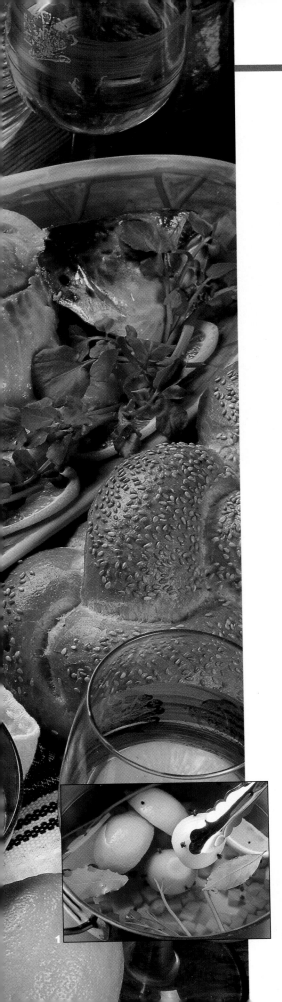

BUFFET

ATLANTIC SALMON WITH DILL MAYONNAISE

Preparation time: 50 minutes
Total cooking time: 50–60 minutes
Serves 8–10

2.5 litres water
2 litres good quality white wine
1/4 cup white wine vinegar
2 onions
10 whole cloves
4 carrots, chopped
1 lemon, cut in quarters
2 bay leaves
1 teaspoon black peppercorns
4 parsley stalks
2.5 kg Atlantic salmon, cleaned
  and scaled

Dill mayonnaise
1 egg
1 egg yolk, extra
1 tablespoon lemon juice
1 teaspoon white wine vinegar
1 1/2 cups light olive oil
1-2 tablespoons fresh chopped
  dill
salt and pepper

➤ PREHEAT OVEN to moderate 180°C. Place water, wine, and vinegar in a large, heavy-based pan.
1 Stud onions with cloves. Add to pan with carrots, lemon, bay leaves, peppercorns and parsley. Bring to boil, reduce heat and simmer 30–35 minutes. Cool. Strain into large baking dish or fish kettle that will hold the salmon.
2 Place the whole, cleaned fish in the baking dish or fish kettle and cover it with foil. Bake 20–30 minutes. Remove fish from the oven and cool.
3 To make Mayonnaise: Place egg and the extra yolk in food processor bowl. Add juice and vinegar. Process 10 seconds or until blended. With motor constantly operating, add oil in a thin, steady stream, blending until all the oil is added and mayonnaise is thick and creamy. Transfer mixture to a small bowl. Add dill, salt and pepper. Mix well. Remove cold fish from liquid. Place on serving platter. Peel back skin. Garnish with watercress and lemon slices. Serve with mayonnaise.

COOK'S FILE

Storage time: Cook the fish several hours before serving. The mayonnaise can be made 2–3 days in advance and refrigerated in an airtight container.
Hint: To ensure mayonnaise thickens properly, have the ingredients at room temperature rather than using them straight from the refrigerator. The mayonnaise should be thick enough to form peaks.
Variation: Olive oil has a strong flavour. Another light vegetable oil may be substituted for it in the mayonnaise recipe.

RENDANG BEEF CURRY

Preparation time: 40 minutes
Total cooking time: 30 minutes
Serves 6–8

5 red dried chillies
2 kg blade or skirt beef
1/4 cup vegetable oil or ghee
2 large onions, 1 thinly sliced,
 1 chopped
10 cm stem lemon grass, cut
 into 3 pieces
4 cloves garlic, peeled
3 cm piece ginger, peeled
2 1/2 cups coconut milk
1 tablespoon ground coriander
1 teaspoon cracked black pepper
1 1/2 teaspoons ground cumin

1 teaspoon turmeric
1/2 teaspoon caraway seeds
2 bay leaves or 10 dried curry
 leaves
1/2 cup coconut cream
sugar and salt to taste

➤ SOAK CHILLIES in boiling water 5-–10 minutes, drain. Remove seeds. Trim meat of excess fat and sinew. Cut meat into thin strips.

1 Heat half the oil or ghee in a large heavy-based pan. Cook meat quickly in small batches over medium-high heat until well browned; drain on sheets of paper towel. Add remaining oil or ghee to pan. Stir in sliced onion. Cook for 5–10 minutes or until well browned. Remove from heat.

2 Place chopped onion, lemon grass, garlic, ginger and drained chillies in food processor. Process until a paste forms. Add paste to pan. Return to stove. Cook, stirring over medium heat, for 3–4 minutes. Add coconut milk and spices. Bring to boil, reduce heat and simmer for 5 minutes.

3 Return meat to pan. Cover, simmer 1 hour. Remove lid, simmer 5–10 minutes more or until liquid reduces. Stir in coconut cream. Season with sugar and salt. Serve with rice and chutney.

COOK'S FILE

Storage time: Make curry up to 2 days in advance. Reheat gently on stove, in oven or in a microwave oven.
Hint: Freeze any leftover coconut milk or cream in ice cube trays. Add to dishes as needed.

FRESH TUNA FETTUCINE

Preparation time: 15 minutes
Total cooking time: 15–20 minutes
Serves 6

750 g fettucine
2 large, ripe tomatoes
125 g fresh asparagus, cut into
    3 cm lengths
1/2 cup olive oil
500 g tuna steaks
3 cloves garlic,
    crushed
2 onions, sliced
1/4 cup finely sliced
    basil leaves
1/4 cup chopped capers

➤ COOK FETTUCINE in a large pan of rapidly boiling salted water until just tender; drain, toss through a little oil to keep strands separate.

1 Prepare ingredients. Peel tomatoes and chop. Cook asparagus in a small pan of rapidly boiling water for 2 minutes or until just tender; drain, rinse under cold water, drain again.

2 Heat 1 tablespoon of the oil in a large frying pan. Add tuna steaks, cook for 2 minutes on each side or until golden brown on the outside but still slightly pink on the inside; remove from pan. Using a fork, shred tuna and remove any bones; set aside.

3 Heat remaining oil in pan. Add the garlic and onions, stir over medium heat for 3 minutes or until onions are tender. Add cooked fettucine, asparagus, tuna, chopped tomatoes, basil and chopped capers; stir over medium heat until all ingredients are combined and heated through.

COOK'S FILE

Storage time: Fettucine, asparagus and tuna can be cooked several hours ahead. Combine with remaining ingredients just before serving.

Hint: A 425 g can of drained, flaked tuna can be used instead of fresh tuna. To peel tomatoes, make a small cross on top, place tomatoes in boiling water for 1–2 minutes, then plunge immediately into cold water. Remove tomatoes and peel off skin downwards from the cross. Chop tomatoes roughly.

CHICKEN AND APRICOT NUT ROLL WITH CREAMY WINE SAUCE

Preparation time: 50 minutes
Total cooking time: 1 hour 55 minutes
+ standing time
Serves 8–10

1/2 cup white short-grain rice
1/2 cup brown rice
1.5 kg double chicken breast
   fillets (about 10 double
   breasts)
100 g macadamia nuts,
   finely chopped
3 teaspoons grated
   fresh ginger
1/3 cup finely chopped
   dried apricots
3 spring onions, chopped
2 tablespoons chopped
   fresh parsley
1 tablespoon chopped fresh
   chives
2 teaspoons chopped fresh
   lemon thyme
3 eggs, lightly beaten
salt and pepper
2 tablespoons olive oil
40 g butter, melted

Creamy wine sauce
60 g butter
8 spring onions, finely chopped
2 tablespoons plain flour
1 cup white wine
1 1/2 cups cream
2 teaspoons Dijon mustard
salt and white pepper to taste

➤ COOK RICES separately in 2 large pans of boiling water until tender, drain well. Set aside to cool.
1 Trim chicken of excess fat and sinew. Lay chicken fillets side-by-side between two large pieces of plastic wrap. Using a rolling pin or meat mallet, pound chicken to a 40 x 40 cm square piece.
2 Preheat oven to moderate 180°C. Combine rices, nuts, ginger, apricots, onions, herbs and eggs in a large mixing bowl. Season to taste with salt and pepper. Spread rice mixture in a log shape towards centre of flattened chicken fillets. Roll up firmly; sprinkle the surface with extra salt and pepper.

3 Wrap chicken roll in a greased sheet of foil; tie securely with string at regular intervals to retain shape. Place on roasting rack in a deep baking dish. Bake 1 hour. Remove foil and string, brush surface of roll with combined oil and melted butter and bake for another 10–15 minutes or until browned on the surface. Cover with foil and stand for 10 minutes before slicing. Slice roll and serve roll hot with Creamy Wine Sauce.
4 To make Creamy Wine Sauce: Melt butter in a small pan and add spring onions. Cook over medium heat for 1 minute. Add flour, stir over heat for 1–2 minutes or until mixture is lightly golden and bubbling. Remove from heat. Add wine and cream gradually, stirring until mixture boils and thickens. Stir in mustard and season with salt and pepper.

COOK'S FILE

Storage: Chicken and apricot roll can be made several hours in advance. Pre-cook and reheat, or bake just before serving. The rice mixture can also be made in advance—add the egg just before spreading mixture on chicken fillets.
Variations: Boneless turkey breast can be substituted for the chicken, if desired. Use almonds to make the filling instead of macadamia nuts— buy slivered almonds and chop finely.

Use chicken stock in place of the wine to make the sauce, or half stock and half wine. Season sauce with herbs instead of mustard, or use a variety of different mustards.

Chicken and apricot nut roll is also delicious cold. Serve sliced, with a dressing made of equal parts mayonnaise and sour cream plus some chopped fresh herbs.
Note: This dish is a crowd pleaser which, even though it takes a little time to prepare, is worth the effort for a party as the result is quite impressive. Guests appreciate the care that has gone into its creation and it is invariably a popular buffet item. Slices are difficult to cut in half as they will lose their filling—you may want to make 2 rolls for anything other than a small gathering, to avoid disappointing some of your guests.

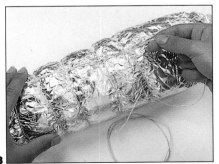

LAMB KORMA

Preparation time: 45 minutes
Total cooking time: 1 hour 30 minutes
Serves 8

1.5 kg lean boneless lamb (leg
   or shoulder)
1/4 cup vegetable oil or ghee
3 large onions, 2 thinly sliced, 1
   sliced in medium-thick rings
1 tablespoon grated ginger
2-3 cloves garlic, crushed
3 teaspoons ground coriander
1 teaspoon mild chilli powder
1/2 teaspoon ground mace
1 cinnamon stick
3 whole cloves
1 1/2 cups plain yoghurt
1 teaspoon salt
1/2 teaspoon cracked black
   pepper
1 1/2 cups water
200 g small button mushrooms,
   sliced
2/3 cup cream
1/2 cup slivered almonds,
   toasted
1/4 cup coriander leaves
oil for deep frying

➤ TRIM MEAT of excess fat and
sinew. Cut into large cubes.

1 Heat oil or ghee in a large heavy-based pan. Cook meat quickly in small batches over medium-high heat until well browned; drain on sheets of paper towel. Add thinly sliced onions. Cook, stirring, until soft. Stir in ginger, garlic, ground coriander, chilli, mace, cinnamon stick and cloves. Cook for 2–3 minutes. Add meat, yoghurt, salt and pepper. Cook, stirring, for another 15 minutes or until yoghurt is absorbed into meat.

2 Pour in water, mix well. Bring to boil, reduce heat, cover and simmer gently for 45 minutes or until meat is almost tender. Stir in mushrooms and cream. Cook, uncovered, 10–20 minutes or until meat is tender. Add almonds just before serving. Garnish with fried onions (see below) and fresh coriander leaves, and serve.

3 To fry onions for garnish: Heat oil in deep heavy-based pan. Cook medium-thick onion rings in moderately hot oil until they turn deep brown and crisp. Remove onion rings from oil with tongs or a slotted spoon and drain on paper towel.

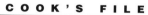

COOK'S FILE

Storage time: Curry tastes better if made a day in advance. Reheat gently before serving. Cook onions for garnishing just before serving. Curry can be frozen, but omit the mushrooms and cream—add when reheating.

Hint: Use a good-quality acidophilus yoghurt for a creamier sauce.

MEDITERRANEAN ROLLS

Preparation time: 1 hour
Total cooking time: 50 minutes
  + refrigeration
Serves 10–15

1 bulb garlic
2 large red capsicum
2 pumpkin wedges (150 g each)
10 rosetta rolls
1/2 bunch English spinach
salt and pepper
250 g mozzarella cheese, thinly
    sliced
1/4 cup olive paste
1 red onion, cut into thin rings
350 g canned or marinated
    artichoke hearts, sliced
20 large basil leaves
60 g sun-dried tomatoes in oil,
    drained, sliced
125 g prosciutto ham, finely
    sliced

➤ PREHEAT OVEN to moderately
hot 210°C. Cut the top from the garlic
bulb. Cut capsicums in half, remove
seed and membrane.
1 Place garlic, capsicum and pumpkin in baking dish. Bake for 50
minutes. Check garlic after 30 minutes, making sure that it is soft and
does not burn. Cut the tops off each
bread roll horizontally. Scoop out
bread from the centres, including
from under the bread 'lids'.
2 Peel the cooked pumpkin wedges
and cut into thin slices. Cover spinach
leaves with boiling water; stand for
1 minute. Drain, squeeze out excess
moisture and pat dry with paper
towel. Peel the skin from capsicum;
cool capsicum completely, then cut
into thin strips. Squeeze cooked garlic
from cloves into a small bowl. Add
salt and pepper to taste and mash

together with a fork. Spread a little
garlic mixture inside each roll.
3 Firmly pack rolls with layers con-
sisting of sliced cooked pumpkin,
spinach leaves, strips of cooked capsicum, sliced cheese, olive paste,
onion rings, sliced artichoke hearts,
basil leaves, sun-dried tomatoes and
slices of prosciutto. Replace lids of
rolls and wrap them tightly in plastic
wrap. Refrigerate for at least 1 hour.
Serve rolls whole or cut in half to
display filling.

Storage time: Mediterranean rolls
are best eaten the day they are made.
Hint: To serve theses rolls warm,
heat in oven for 10–15 minutes.
Variation: Hollowed out rosetta rolls
make good cases for any favourite
cooked meat, seafood, vegetable or
salad fillings that are not so moist as
to make the bread go soggy.
Note: Mediterranean Rolls will carry
well and are a delicious addition to a
picnic hamper.

1

2

3

CHICKEN IN ASPARAGUS SAUCE

Preparation time: 1 hour
Total cooking time: 1 hour 20 minutes
Serves 6–8

2 kg chicken thigh fillets
60 g butter
2 tablespoons olive oil
3 onions, thinly sliced
1 cup dry white wine
1¹/₂ cups chicken stock
salt and pepper
2 x 340 g cans asparagus
   spears, puréed
1 cup cream
60 g butter, extra
¹/₃ cup plain flour

1 cup grated cheddar cheese
¹/₃ cup grated parmesan cheese
2¹/₄ cups breadcrumbs (made
   from stale bread)

➤ PREHEAT OVEN to moderate 180°C. Trim chicken of excess fat and sinew. Cut into cubes.

1 Heat half the butter and oil in a large heavy-based pan. Cook chicken in small batches over medium-high heat until well browned. Drain on sheets of paper towel.

2 Add remaining butter and oil to pan. Stir in onion. Cook until softened. Remove from pan. Pour in wine. Bring to boil, stir to mix in pan juices. Add stock, salt, pepper, chicken and onion. Bring to boil, reduce heat. Simmer, covered, 10 minutes or until chicken is tender. Combine puréed asparagus and cream in a large jug. Add to chicken mixture. Beat extra butter and flour together until smooth, add to pan in small amounts. Stir over medium heat for 5 minutes or until mixture boils and thickens. Cook, simmering, for 30–40 minutes.

3 Transfer mixture to a large casserole dish. Scatter over combined cheeses and breadcrumbs. Bake for 25–30 minutes or until golden brown on top. Serve hot.

COOK'S FILE

Storage time: Make casserole up to a day in advance. Sprinkle the cheese mixture over it before reheating.
Variation: Add a pinch of cayenne pepper to topping for a spicy touch.

HERBED FILLET OF BEEF

Preparation time: 30 minutes
Total cooking time: 1 hour 25 minutes
Serves 8–10

2 kg beef fillet
2 teaspoons ground black
    pepper
50 g butter
1/2 cup light olive oil
1/4 cup virgin olive oil
2 tablespoons white wine
    vinegar
2 tablespoons French mustard
2 tablespoons mayonnaise
2 teaspoons worcestershire
    sauce
1 tablespoon chopped capers

1/4 cup finely chopped fresh
    chives
1/4 cup finely chopped fresh
    parsley
1 teaspoon finely chopped fresh
    thyme
2 teaspoons finely chopped
    fresh marjoram
45 g parmesan cheese, shaved

➤ PREHEAT OVEN to moderately
hot 210°C (190°C gas). Trim meat of
excess fat and sinew. Tie meat securely with string at regular intervals to
retain its shape. Rub meat all over
with pepper.
1 Heat butter in large heavy-based
frying pan. Cook meat over medium-
high heat until all sides are browned.
Place meat in large baking dish. Bake

1 hour–1 1/4 hours. Remove from oven.
Wrap in foil, then in a tea-towel. Cool
and refrigerate for up to 24 hours.
2 Combine oils and vinegar in a jug
then divide between two bowls. Add
mustard and mayonnaise to one bowl
and worcestershire sauce, capers and
herbs to the other. Mix each well.
3 Cut beef into thin slices. Pour mayonnaise dressing onto serving platter
with a lip. Arrange overlapping slices
of beef on top. Drizzle with herb
dressing and sprinkle with cheese
shavings. Serve.

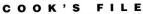

COOK'S FILE

Storage time: Once the beef is
dressed it is best served within the
hour. Dressings can be made up to 12
hours in advance.

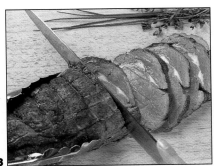

SMOKED COD AND SPINACH ROULADE

Preparation time: 45 minutes
Total cooking time: 20 minutes
Makes 12 slices

500 g bunch English spinach
(about 8 large leaves)
1/2 cup chopped parsley
125 g butter
2/3 cup plain flour
2 cups milk
4 eggs, separated

Filling
400 g smoked cod
250 g ricotta cheese
2 tablespoons chopped fresh
chives
1 tablespoon chopped fresh dill
1 tablespoon seeded mustard
1 tablespoon lemon juice

➤ PREHEAT OVEN to moderately hot 210°C (gas 190°C). Brush a 30 x 25 x 2 cm shallow Swiss roll tin with melted butter or oil. Cover the base with paper, extending over two sides; grease paper. Remove stalks from the spinach leaves and discard. Chop leaves roughly, blanch in boiling water for 2 minutes or until tender. Rinse under cold water, drain and squeeze out liquid. Combine spinach and parsley in a food processor bowl. Blend for 10 seconds or until very finely chopped. Set aside.

1 Melt butter in a medium pan and add flour. Stir over low heat for one minute; remove from heat. Add the milk gradually to the pan, stirring until mixture is smooth. Return to stove. Stir constantly over medium heat for 2 minutes or until mixture boils and thickens; boil for 1 minute more, then remove from heat. Divide mixture in half, reserving one half for filling. Stir spinach mixture and egg yolks into the other half.

2 Place egg whites in a small, dry, mixing bowl. Using electric beaters, beat egg whites until stiff peaks form. Using a metal spoon, gently fold into the spinach mixture.

3 Spread the mixture evenly into prepared tin and smooth the surface. Bake for 12 minutes or until a light golden colour. Remove from oven and turn onto a dry tea-towel which has been covered with a sheet of grease-proof paper. Peel paper used to line tin from the surface of the roulade. Using the tea-towel as a guide, carefully roll up from the narrow side, along with greaseproof paper (paper must be rolled up inside to stop roulade sticking to itself). Leave for 3 minutes; unroll roulade and remove the paper.

4 To make Filling: Place the cod in a medium pan, cover with water and bring to the boil. Reduce heat to low and simmer for 3 minutes or until cod is tender. Drain and cool. Flake the cod with a fork and remove any bones. Combine reserved mixture in a large bowl with the ricotta, chives, dill, mustard and lemon juice. Add cod and stir until combined. Spread filling evenly over flattened roulade and roll up again. Refrigerate until firm. Slice and serve.

COOK'S FILE

Storage time: Roulade can be made a day ahead. Store, covered, in the refrigerator. For the best texture, let the roulade stand for at least 30 minutes at room temperature before slicing and serving.
Variation: Canned tuna or salmon, drained and flaked, or flaked, poached fresh fish such as schnapper or perch, can be used instead of the cod. Use 1/2 packet frozen spinach, thawed and with excess moisture squeezed out, instead of fresh. Use silverbeet if English spinach is unavailable. Softened cream cheese or cottage cheese can be substituted for ricotta.

Because this dish is actually a spinach soufflé with smoked cod filling, it is very light and would make a good first course for a dinner party. Give each guest one or two slices, depending on the course to follow. It can also be served as a light lunch dish, with a salad and crusty bread.
Note: Roulade is first rolled up with greaseproof paper so that it will form a curved shape while still warm and pliable, without the surface cracking. When unrolled, it should retain the curve enough to be successfully re-rolled with filling inside. The tea-towel is used to assist with handling the delicate surface.

2

3

4

BEEF LASAGNE

Preparation time: 45 minutes
Total cooking time: 45 minutes
Serves 16

1 tablespoon oil
1.5 kg beef mince
2 tablespoons oil, extra
2 onions, chopped
2 medium zucchini, chopped
250 g baby mushrooms, sliced
750 g bottle ready-made tomato
    pasta sauce
2 x 410 g cans tomato pieces
2 x 140 g cans tomato paste
1 tablespoon caster sugar
1 cup red wine
salt and pepper
2 x 250 g packets instant
    lasagne sheets

Cream sauce
125 g butter
2/3 cup plain flour
6 cups milk
salt and pepper
150 g cheddar cheese, grated
1/4 cup grated parmesan cheese

➤ PREHEAT OVEN to moderate 180°C. Grease two 20 x 35 x 7 cm baking dishes.

1 Heat oil in large pan, cook mince in batches until browned. Transfer to bowl. Heat extra oil in the same pan, cook onion until soft. Add zucchini and mushrooms, cook until just tender. Return meat to onion mixture, add pasta sauce, undrained tomato pieces, tomato paste, sugar, wine, and salt and pepper. Simmer, covered, for 30 minutes, stirring occasionally. Remove from heat and set aside.

2 To make Sauce: Heat butter in medium pan until melted. Add flour, cook, stirring over heat until mixture bubbles. Remove from heat, add milk gradually to pan, stirring, until smooth. Stir over heat until sauce boils and thickens. Add salt, pepper and cheese. Mix until smooth and cheese has melted.

3 To assemble: Spread half a cup of tomato mixture over base of each baking dish. Top with lasagne sheets to cover. Spread one-sixth of the cheese sauce over pasta. Spread each with a quarter of the tomato sauce. Repeat layering with pasta, cream sauce, then tomato sauce, finishing with a pasta sheet topped with cream sauce. Sprinkle with extra grated cheese. Bake 45 minutes or until cooked through and lightly browned.

COOKS FILE

Storage time: Cover and refrigerate for up to 2 days. Lasagne can be stored, frozen, for up to 2 months.
Hint: Fresh lasagne sheets can be used in this recipe. You will need two 375 g packets of fresh lasagne sheets.

PRAWN MANGO SALAD

Preparation time: 25 minutes
Total cooking time: 5 minutes
Serves 10–12

2 kg cooked king prawns
6 rashers bacon, chopped
3 large mangoes, peeled, or 2 x
    425 g cans mangoes in
    syrup, drained
2 large avocados

Dressing
2 tablespoons sour cream
170 g can mango puree
¼ cup lime juice
1 tablespoon Thai sweet chilli
    sauce
salt and pepper to taste

➤ CHECK PRAWNS are firm.
1 Peel prawns, removing heads and
leaving tails intact.
2 Cook bacon in medium pan until
crisp; drain on paper towel. Cut mangoes into thin wedges. Peel avocados,
remove seeds, cut into slices. Arrange
prawns, mangoes and avocado on
large platter. Sprinkle with bacon.
Drizzle with dressing before serving.
3 To make Dressing: Combine all
ingredients in a small bowl and whisk
until smooth.

COOK'S FILE

Storage time: Peel prawns and
make dressing several hours ahead.
Assemble just before serving.

ASIAN-STYLE PASTA SALAD

Preparation time: 30 minutes
Total cooking time: 6–8 minutes
Serves 10–15

3 x 375 g packs fresh tri-
  coloured tortellini
1 Lebanese cucumber
1 carrot
150 g snow peas
2 sticks celery
4 spring onions, sliced
1/2 Chinese cabbage,
  shredded
1 red capsicum, sliced

Dressing
3/4 cup orange juice
1/3 cup lemon juice
1/4 cup soy sauce
1/4 cup sesame oil
1/4 cup honey
2 tablespoons sweet Thai chilli
  sauce

➤ BRING A LARGE PAN of salted
water to the boil.
1 Add the pasta and cook until just
tender; drain and rinse under cold
water. Place in a large serving bowl.
2 Cut cucumber, carrot, and snow
peas into thin matchstick strips about
6 cm long. Cut the celery diagonally
into thin slices. Add the carrot,
cucumber, snowpeas, celery, spring
onions, cabbage and capsicum to the
pasta. Mix well.
3 To make Dressing: Combine
juices, soy sauce, oil, honey and chilli
sauce in a screw-top jar; shake well.
Just before serving, pour dressing
over the pasta salad and toss well to
combine .

COOKS FILE

Storage time: Pasta and dressing
can be prepared a day ahead; cover
each and store separately in the
refrigerator.
Hint: Fresh tortellini, with either
meat or cheese and spinach filling, is
available from most supermarkets.

SEAFOOD MORNAY

Preparation time: 35 minutes
Total cooking time: 35 minutes
Serves 8–10

60 g butter
1/2 cup plain flour
2/3 cup dry white wine
1 cup thick cream
3/4 cup milk
salt and pepper to taste
1 cup grated cheddar cheese
2 tablespoons seeded mustard
1 tablespoon horseradish cream
6 spring onions, chopped
20 g butter, extra

450 g scallops
1 kg boneless white fish fillets
400 g cooked peeled prawns
2 cups fresh breadcrumbs

Topping
3 cups fresh breadcrumbs
1/4 cup chopped fresh parsley
60 g butter, melted
1 cup grated cheddar cheese

➤ PREHEAT OVEN to moderate 180°C. Lightly grease an 8-cup capacity baking dish. Cut fish into cubes.
1 Melt butter in medium pan. Add flour, bring to boil, stirring. Reduce heat, stir in wine, cream and milk. Stir over high heat until sauce boils and thickens. Season with salt and pepper. Add cheese, mustard, horseradish and onions; mix well. Set aside.
2 Heat extra butter in large pan, add seafood in batches. Stir over low heat until liquid starts to seep from seafood. Drain seafood, add to sauce. Add breadcrumbs; mix well. Place mixture in prepared baking dish.
3 To make Topping: Combine all ingredients, mix well. Spread over seafood mixture. Bake for 35 minutes or until topping is golden and sauce bubbling.

COOKS FILE

Storage time: Can be prepared a day ahead and stored in refrigerator.

BACON AND EGG QUICHE

Preparation time: 30 minutes
Total cooking time: 1 hour 5 minutes +
standing time
Serves 10–12

Pastry
1¹/₂ cups plain flour
100 g butter, chopped
1 egg
1 tablespoon water,
approximately

Filling
10 thinly sliced bacon rashers
6 eggs
²/₃ cup milk
1¹/₄ cups thick cream
salt and pepper
¹/₂ cup grated cheddar cheese

➤ PREHEAT OVEN to moderately hot 210°C.

1 To make Pastry: Place flour and butter in bowl of food processor. Using pulse action, press button for 30 seconds or until mixture is fine and crumbly. Add egg and water, process 20 seconds or until mixture just comes together when squeezed. Turn onto a lightly floured board. Knead mixture gently to form a smooth dough. Refrigerate, covered with plastic wrap, for 20 minutes.

2 Roll pastry on a floured board large enough to fit a 32 cm round loose-bottomed flan tin. Ease pastry into tin. Trim edge with a rolling pin. Cut a sheet of baking paper to cover pastry lined tin. Line with paper; spread a layer of dried beans or rice evenly over paper. Bake for 15 minutes, remove paper and beans; bake for another 10 minutes or until pastry case is lightly browned; cool. Reduce

oven temperature to moderate 180°C.

3 To make Filling: Reserve 4 slices of bacon. Chop remaining bacon rashers. Heat pan, cook bacon until crisp; drain on paper towel. Combine eggs, milk, cream, salt and pepper in large jug. Whisk well. Put bacon into pastry case, pour over cream mixture. Cut reserved bacon in halves. Lay

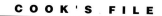

strips over top, sprinkle with cheese. Bake for 40 minutes or until cooked through and golden on top. Serve warm.

COOK'S FILE

Storage time: Pastry for the quiche can be made a day ahead. The cooked quiche can be frozen.

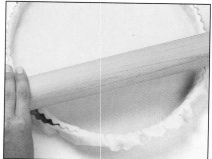

CHICKEN CURRY

Preparation time: 20 minutes
Total cooking time: 35–40 minutes
Serves 10–12

2 kg chicken thigh fillets
3/4 cup plain flour
2 tablespoons oil
3 onions, chopped
2 teaspoons finely grated ginger
3 cloves garlic, crushed
3 teaspoons turmeric
2-3 teaspoons chilli powder
2 teaspoons ground coriander
2 teaspoons ground cumin

1 teaspoon ground cinnamon
1 3/4 cups chicken stock
3 green apples
1 cup sultanas
1/2 cup desiccated coconut
400 ml can coconut cream

➤ TRIM CHICKEN of excess fat and sinew and cut into 2.5 cm cubes.
1 Toss chicken in flour, shake off excess. Heat oil in large pan, cook fillets in batches until well browned; remove from pan. Add onion to same pan, cook, stirring, until soft. Add ginger, garlic, turmeric, chilli powder, coriander, cumin and cinnamon. Cook, stirring, until fragrant.

2 Return chicken to pan with chicken stock. Simmer, covered, 15 minutes.
3 Peel and core apples. Cut into 1 cm cubes. Add apples, sultanas, coconut and coconut cream to pan. Simmer, uncovered, stirring occasionally, for 15 minutes. Serve with rice.

COOK'S FILE

Storage time: This curry can be made several hours or even a day ahead. Store, covered, in refrigerator.
Hint: Curry can be served with small bowls of accompaniments such as chopped tomatoes, crushed peanuts, sliced banana and desiccated coconut, if desired.

1

2

3

SIDE DISHES

GRILLED VEGETABLES WITH GARLIC MAYONNAISE

Preparation time: 30 minutes
Total cooking time: 15 minutes
Serves 8

2 medium eggplants, cut into
    thin slices
salt
4 small leeks, halved
    lengthways
2 medium red capsicums
4 small zucchini, halved
    lengthways
8 large flat mushrooms

Dressing
1 tablespoon balsamic
    vinegar
2 tablespoons Dijon
    mustard
2 teaspoons dried oregano
    leaves
1 cup olive oil

Garlic Mayonnaise
2 egg yolks
1 tablespoon lemon juice
2 cloves garlic, crushed
1 cup olive oil
1 tablespoon chopped fresh
    chives
1 tablespoon chopped fresh
    parsley
1 tablespoon water

➤ SPRINKLE EGGPLANT slices with salt, allow to stand for 30 minutes. Rinse under cold water, pat dry with paper towel.

1 Cut capsicum into eighths.

2 Place eggplant, leek, capsicum and zucchini in a single layer on a flat grill tray, brush with dressing. Cook, under pre-heated grill, on high for 5 minutes; brush occasionally with dressing. Add mushrooms, cap side up, to grill tray, brush with dressing. Continue to cook vegetables for 10 minutes or until tender, turn mushrooms only once. Brush vegetables with dressing during cooking. Serve with Garlic Mayonnaise.

To make Dressing: Combine vinegar, mustard and oregano in a small bowl, gradually whisk in oil.

3 To make Garlic Mayonnaise: Place egg yolks, lemon juice and garlic in a food processor bowl or blender, blend for 5 seconds until combined. With motor constantly operating, add oil slowly in a thin, steady stream until all oil is added and mayonnaise is thick and creamy. Add chives, parsley and water, blend for 3 seconds until combined.

COOK'S FILE

Storage time: Garlic mayonnaise can be made several days ahead; store in the refrigerator. Cook vegetables just before serving.

Hint: Do not worry if dressing separates—simply brush on as required.

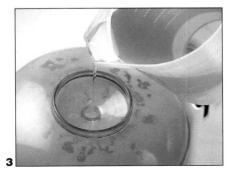

CHEESY SUN-DRIED TOMATO HOT BREAD

Preparation time: 15 minutes
Total cooking time: 15 minutes
Serves 10

60 g butter, softened
1/3 cup grated parmesan cheese
2 tablespoons sun-dried tomato
　　paste
1 tablespoon chopped basil
2 French bread sticks

➤ PREHEAT OVEN to moderately hot 210°C (190°C gas).

1 Combine butter, cheese, sun-dried tomato paste and basil in a small mixing bowl.

2 Slice bread almost through at 1.5 cm intervals, leaving base intact. Spread butter mixture between the slices, then press back into loaf shape.

3 Wrap bread in foil. Bake for 10 minutes, open foil and bake for another 5 minutes or until bread is crisp.

COOK'S FILE:

Storage time: Bread sticks can be assembled several hours ahead; bake them just before serving. Prepared unbaked bread sticks can be frozen for up to 2 months.

Hint: Sun-dried tomato paste is available from most delicatessens.

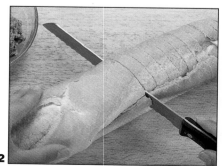

CAESAR SALAD

Preparation time: 30 minutes
Total cooking time: 10 minutes
Serves 10

4 slices bread
2 tablespoons oil
8 rashers bacon, chopped
cos lettuce, leaves torn
2/3 cup shaved parmesan
    cheese

Dressing
1 egg
1/3 cup oil
2 teaspoons white wine vinegar
3 teaspoons Dijon mustard

1 canned anchovy, drained,
    chopped
1 clove garlic, crushed

➤ PREHEAT OVEN to moderately hot 210°C (190°C gas).

1 Remove bread crusts, cut bread into small cubes. Place in a shallow baking dish, bake for 10 minutes or until golden brown, tossing occasionally.

2 Heat oil in a frying pan. Add bacon and stir over medium heat for 3 minutes or until bacon is crisp. Drain on paper towel. Combine bread, bacon, lettuce and cheese in a bowl. Add dressing, toss until combined.

3 To make Dressing: Lower egg into a pan of boiling water and cook for 1 minute; drain. Place remaining dressing ingredients into a food processor bowl or blender. Add egg and blend for 1 minute or until dressing is smooth.

COOK'S FILE

Storage time: Bread cubes can be made several days ahead and stored in an airtight container. The bacon can be fried several hours ahead. Dressing can be made several days ahead; cover and store in the refrigerator but return to room temperature before use. Assemble the salad just before serving.

Hint: Any remaining dressing can be stored in the refrigerator in a small screw-top jar for up to 2 days. Use with other salads.

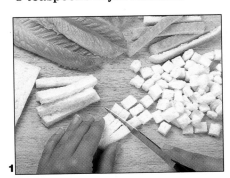

PASTA AND BROCCOLI SALAD WITH AVOCADO DRESSING

Preparation time: 20 minutes
Total cooking time: 10 minutes
Serves 8

250 g tricolour spiral pasta
250 g broccoli
2/3 cup slivered almonds, toasted
2 spring onions, very finely sliced
1/4 cup thinly sliced basil leaves

Avocado Dressing
1/2 large, ripe avocado
2 tablespoons water
1 tablespoon plain yoghurt
1 tablespoon oil
1 teaspoon tarragon vinegar
1 clove garlic, crushed

➤ COOK PASTA in a large pan of rapidly boiling salted water with a little oil added until just tender; drain, rinse under cold water, drain again.

1 Cut broccoli into tiny florets, add to a pan of boiling water. Cook for 3 minutes or until just tender; drain, rinse under cold water, drain again.

2 To make Avocado Dressing: Combine all ingredients for the dressing in a blender or food processor bowl. Blend for 30 seconds or until smooth.

3 Combine pasta and broccoli in a large bowl with almonds, spring onions and basil. Add avocado dressing; stir until combined.

COOK'S FILE

Storage time: Avocado dressing can be made several hours ahead. Completely cover surface of dressing with plastic wrap and store in refrigerator. Both pasta and broccoli can be prepared several hours ahead of time. Combine the ingredients just before serving.

Hint: To toast almonds, spread on a baking tray, bake in moderate (180°C) oven 10 minutes or until golden brown; or place in a frying pan, stir over moderate heat until golden.

MEDITERRANEAN SALAD

Preparation time: 40 minutes
Total cooking time: 2 minutes
Serves 8

1 medium eggplant
salt
2 tablespoons oil
250 g punnet cherry tomatoes,
    halved
2 Lebanese cucumbers, sliced
1 red onion, very thinly sliced
250 g feta cheese, cut into 2 cm
    cubes
$^2/_3$ cup pitted black olives
$^1/_3$ cup finely chopped basil
    leaves

Dressing
$^1/_3$ cup olive oil
1 tablespoon balsamic vinegar
1 clove garlic, crushed
1 tablespoon chopped oregano
    leaves

➤ CUT EGGPLANT into 2.5 cm
cubes and spread out on a plate.
1 Sprinkle with a little salt and let
stand for 30 minutes. Rinse under
cold water, pat dry with paper towel.
2 Heat oil in a shallow pan, add eggplant. Stir over medium heat for
2 minutes or until eggplant is lightly
browned and tender; drain on paper
towel, cool. Combine eggplant in a
large bowl with tomatoes, cucumber,
onion, cheese, olives and basil.
3 To make Dressing: Place all
ingredients in a small screwtop jar.
Shake vigorously for 10 seconds. Add
to salad, toss until mixed well.

COOK'S FILE

Storage time: Both salad and dressing can be made several hours ahead.
Combine just before serving.

1

2

3

HERB AND GARLIC CORNBREAD SLICES

Preparation time: 20 minutes
Total cooking time: 50 minutes
Makes about 16 slices

2/3 cup self-raising flour
2 teaspoons baking
    powder
1/2 teaspoon chilli
    powder
1 1/2 cups polenta (fine)
90 g butter, melted
3 eggs, lightly beaten
3/4 cup milk

Herb and Garlic Butter
125 g butter, softened
1 tablespoon chopped parsley
1 tablespoon chopped chives
2 cloves garlic, crushed

➤ PREHEAT OVEN to moderate 180°C. Brush a 21 x 14 x 7 cm loaf tin with melted butter or oil; line base and sides with baking paper.
1 Sift flour, baking powder and chilli into a large mixing bowl. Add polenta and stir until combined. Make a well in the centre. Add butter, eggs and milk to dry ingredients. Using a wooden spoon, stir until just combined; do not overbeat the mixture.

2 Pour mixture into prepared tin. Bake for 45 minutes or until bread is firm in the centre and beginning to brown around the edges. Turn bread out onto a wire rack, stand at least 10 minutes or until cool. Using a sharp knife, cut loaf into thin slices.
3 To make Herb and Garlic Butter: Combine all ingredients. Spread on cornbread slices. Place slices on oven tray; bake for another 5 minutes or until slightly crispy.

COOK'S FILE

Storage time: Unbuttered cornbread slices will keep for up to 3 days in an airtight container.

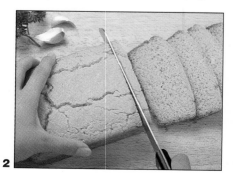

THAI POTATO SALAD

Preparation time: 15 minutes
Total cooking time: 5 minutes
Serves 8

1 kg baby potatoes

Dressing
1 clove garlic
1/4 cup lime juice
2 tablespoons oil
2 tablespoons chopped fresh
    mint
2 tablespoons chopped fresh
    coriander

1 tablespoon Thai fish sauce
2 teaspoons sweet Thai chilli
    sauce
1 teaspoon sugar

➤ SCRUB POTATOES under cold water.
1 Cut potatoes in half and cook in boiling water for 5 minutes or until just tender. Drain, rinse under cold water and allow to cool.
2 To make Dressing: Crush clove of garlic into a bowl. Transfer to a small screwtop jar, add lime juice, oil, mint, coriander.
3 Add sauces and sugar to screwtop jar; shake for 30 seconds to combine

ingredients. Place potatoes in a bowl, pour dressing over and combine well.

COOK'S FILE

Storage time: Thai potato salad can be made a day ahead; store, covered, in the refrigerator. Toss ingredients well just before serving
Variation: Potatoes of any variety, cut into cubes, can be used for this recipe if desired. Add 2 teaspoons finely chopped lemongrass and extra chopped fresh chilli to dressing.
Hint: If using cubed potatoes, be careful not to overcook them or potato salad will become mushy when dressing is added.

POTATO AND KUMARA GRATIN WITH THYME

Preparation time: 15 minutes
Total cooking time: 45–50 minutes
Serves 8

2 tablespoons oil
2 leeks, chopped
2 cloves garlic, crushed
1 tablespoon chopped fresh
    thyme

3/4 cup cream
3/4 cup chicken stock
500 g potatoes
500 g kumara (orange sweet
    potato)
1/3 cup finely grated gruyère
    cheese

➤ PREHEAT OVEN to moderately hot 210°C (190°C gas).

1 Heat oil in frying pan, add leeks, garlic and thyme, stir over low heat 4 minutes or until soft. Add cream and stock, bring to boil; remove from heat.

2 Peel and thinly slice potato and kumara. Place in alternating layers in shallow 8-cup ovenproof dish. Pour over cream mixture, spreading leeks with a spoon. Sprinkle cheese on top.

3 Bake for 45 minutes or until golden brown and potatoes are just tender.

COOK'S FILE

Storage time: Cream mixture can be made ahead of time. Prepare potatoes and kumara just before cooking.

NUTTY FRIED RICE

Preparation time: 30 minutes
Total cooking time: 40–50 minutes
Serves 8–10

1 cup brown rice
2 cups long grain white rice
1 tablespoon sesame oil
1 large onion, finely
    chopped
2 cloves garlic, crushed
2 sticks celery, finely sliced
    diagonally
1 large carrot, finely chopped
60 g bamboo shoots, drained,
    sliced
4 spring onions, finely sliced

150 g Chinese barbecue pork,
    chopped
150 g cooked school prawns,
    peeled
1/2 cup roasted peanuts
1/4 cup coriander leaves
1 tablespoon soy sauce
salt and pepper to taste

➤ COOK BROWN rice in large pan of rapidly boiling water 20–30 minutes or until tender. Drain well. Set aside.

1 Place white rice in large heavy-based pan. Add cold water, ensure there is 3 cm of water on top of the rice. Cover with tight-fitting lid. Bring water slowly to the boil; stir once. Reduce heat; simmer, covered, 10–15 minutes or until water is absorbed.

Remove from heat, stand 5–10 minutes. Transfer to large bowl to cool.

2 Heat oil in large wok or frying pan. Add onion and cook over medium heat 3–4 minutes until soft. Add garlic, celery, carrot, bamboo shoots, spring onions, pork and prawns. Cook, stirring, for 3–4 minutes.

3 Add rice, peanuts, coriander, soy sauce, salt and pepper. Toss to combine. Cook until all ingredients are warmed. Serve.

COOK'S FILE

Storage: Rice may be cooked 2–3 hours in advance. Reheat gently to serve, or serve cold.

Hint: Add 1 tablespoon sweet chilli sauce for a spicier flavour.

GADO GADO WITH PEANUT DRESSING

Preparation time: 30 minutes
Total cooking time: 10–15 minutes
Serves 8–10

750 g baby potatoes
200 g green beans
1 large carrot
2 Lebanese cucumbers
4 hard-boiled eggs
250 g punnet cherry tomatoes
250 g bean sprouts
4 spring onions, cut diagonally
        into 2 cm pieces
500 g Chinese cabbage, roughly
        chopped (optional)

Peanut Dressing
2-3 tablespoons peanut oil
1 medium onion, finely chopped
2 cloves garlic, crushed
1/3 cup smooth peanut butter
3 teaspoons soy sauce
1 tablespoon soft brown sugar
1/2-1 teaspoon chilli paste
1 teaspoon lemon juice
1 1/4 cups thick coconut milk
salt and pepper to taste

➤ HALVE POTATOES; microwave
or boil until just tender. Cool.
1 Trim tops from beans. Cut carrot
into thin sticks. Steam or microwave
beans and carrots until tender, then
immediately plunge into a bowl of iced
water. Drain and set aside.
2 Cut cucumber into sticks. Cut eggs
into quarters. Arrange all vegetables
and eggs on serving platter and serve
with Peanut Dressing.
3 To make Peanut Dressing: Heat
oil in medium heavy-based pan. Add
onion and garlic. Cook over medium
heat 2–3 minutes or until onion is soft.
Add peanut butter, soy sauce, sugar,

chilli, juice. Cook, stirring, 1 minute.
Add coconut milk. Stir over medium
heat 3–4 minutes until smooth and
heated through. Season with salt and
pepper. Remove from heat. Serve
warm or cold with vegetable platter.

COOK'S FILE

Storage time: Make Peanut Dressing
several hours in advance and reheat
gently to serve.
Hint: You can use any selection of
vegetables for this recipe.

1

2

3

CITRUS WALNUT SALAD

Preparation time: 20 minutes
Total cooking time: Nil
Serves 8

2 oranges
2 grapefruit
125 g sugar snap peas
1/2 bunch rocket,
   leaves torn
1/2 oak leaf lettuce,
   leaves torn
1 large Lebanese cucumber, sliced
1/3 cup walnut pieces

Walnut Dressing
2 tablespoons walnut oil
2 tablespoons oil
2 teaspoons tarragon vinegar
2 teaspoons seeded mustard
1 teaspoon sweet chilli sauce

➤ PEEL ORANGES and grapefruit, removing all white pith.
1 Segment fruit, remove seeds. Cover sugar snap peas with boiling water; stand 2 minutes. Plunge peas into iced water. Drain and pat dry with sheets of paper towel. Combine fruit, peas, lettuce, cucumber and walnut pieces in a large bowl.

2 To make Walnut Dressing: Combine all ingredients in a screw-top jar and shake well.
3 Pour dressing over salad ingredients and toss until combined.

COOK'S FILE

Storage time: Salad ingredients and dressing can be prepared several hours ahead. Shake dressing well and add just before serving.
Hint: Any lettuce leaves of your choice are suitable for this recipe. Walnut oil is available from delicatessens and can also be found at most health food stores.

DESSERTS

LAYERED PASSIONFRUIT TORTE

Preparation time: 45 minutes
Total cooking time: 25 minutes
Makes one 23 cm round cake

6 eggs, separated
3/4 cup sugar
1/2 teaspoon vanilla essence
1/2 cup cornflour
1 1/2 teaspoons baking powder
1/4 cup plain flour

Filling
1 tablespoon lemon juice
1 tablespoon gelatine
1/4 cup water
pulp of 10 passionfruit
500 g cream cheese
1 1/2 cups icing sugar, sifted
3/4 cup cream, lightly whipped
1/2 cup cream, extra, whipped to
   stiff peaks
pulp of 2 passionfruit, extra
1/4 cup roasted almonds or
   pistachios, chopped

➤ PREHEAT OVEN to moderate 180°C. Brush two shallow 23 cm round cake tins with oil or melted butter. Line bases with baking paper.
1 Place egg whites in a large dry mixing bowl. Beat with electric beaters until stiff peaks form. Add sugar gradually, beating until all the sugar has dissolved and mixture is thick and glossy. Fold in yolks and essence. Sift over dry ingredients, gently fold in until mixture is smooth. Spoon mixture evenly into prepared tins. Bake for 20 minutes or until cakes shrink away from sides of tins. Stand 5 minutes before turning them onto wire racks to cool.

2 To make Filling: Combine the juice, gelatine and water in a small bowl. Heat half the passionfruit pulp in a small pan until it boils. Add the gelatine mixture. Stir over medium heat until dissolved. Strain the mixture through a sieve and add to remaining passionfruit pulp. Cool slightly. Beat the cream cheese and sugar with electric beaters until mixture is smooth and creamy. Add the passionfruit mixture. Fold in the lightly whipped cream.

3 To assemble Cake: Cut each cake in half horizontally. Place one layer on serving plate and spread with one fifth of filling. Continue layering, leaving enough filling to spread evenly over top and sides of cake. Pipe rosettes of extra whipped cream around top edge of cake. Spread extra passionfruit pulp over top. Sprinkle nuts over rosettes. Refrigerate for several hours.

COOK'S FILE

Storage time: This dessert cake can be assembled up to three days in advance. Add rosettes and pulp just before serving.

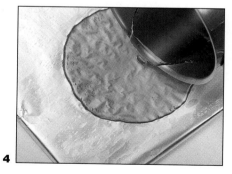

APPLE LEMON BAVAROIS WITH TOFFEE

Preparation time: 50 minutes
Total cooking time: 15–20 minutes
Serves 6–8

1 kg green apples
2 teaspoons grated lemon rind
1/4 cup soft brown sugar
2 tablespoons apricot jam
2 tablespoons water
1 tablespoon gelatine
2 tablespoons water, extra
3 eggs
1/2 cup caster sugar
1 tablespoon orange liqueur
3/4 cup cream, whipped to firm peaks

Toffee
3/4 cup sugar
1/4 cup water

Topping
1 cup cream
2 teaspoons grated orange rind
2 tablespoons orange liqueur

➤ PEEL, CORE and thinly slice apples. Place slices in large pan.

1 Add rind, brown sugar, jam and water to pan and stir. Cover and cook over low heat 5–10 minutes or until apples become very soft. Cool slightly.

2 Process apple mixture until smooth. Sprinkle gelatine over extra water in small bowl. Stand in boiling water, stir until dissolved. Add to apple mixture; process well.

3 Separate 2 eggs and place yolks in a bowl with remaining whole egg and caster sugar. Beat with electric beaters until thick and pale. Fold in apple mixture and liqueur. Beat egg whites in a dry bowl until stiff peaks form. Using a metal spoon, fold egg whites and cream into apple mixture. Spoon into 3/4-cup capacity ramekin dishes. Place ramekins on tray and refrigerate for up to 12 hours. Decorate bavarois with topping and sprinkle with crushed toffee.

4 **To make Toffee:** Combine sugar and water in small pan. Stir over low heat without boiling, until sugar dissolves. Bring to boil, reduce heat and simmer 5–10 minutes or until golden brown. Pour onto an oiled foil-lined tray. Allow to harden. Lightly crush.

To make Topping: Combine cream and rind in bowl. Beat until firm peaks form. Fold in liqueur.

COOK'S FILE

Storage time: Make up to 1 day ahead. Decorate before serving.

Hint: Serve individual bavarois accompanied by a sponge finger or sweet biscuit.

TROPICAL FRUIT SALAD WITH GINGER SYRUP

Preparation time: 40 minutes
Total cooking time: 10–15 minutes
Serves 8–10

Ginger Syrup
rind of 1 lemon or lime
2 tablespoons lemon or lime juice
3/4 cup water
1/3 cup sugar
2 tablespoons finely shredded
    ginger
pulp of 2 passionfruit
2 large mangoes

1 large pawpaw
1 small pineapple
3 bananas
2 star fruit
6 fresh lychees, peeled

➤ THINLY PEEL STRIPS of rind from lemon or lime.

1 To make Syrup: Combine rind, juice, water and sugar in a medium pan. Stir over medium heat without boiling until sugar dissolves. Bring to boil; add the ginger. Reduce heat, simmer for 10 minutes. Remove mixture from heat, cool. Strain syrup, discard rind and ginger. Stir passionfruit pulp into syrup.

2 Peel mangoes and pawpaw, remove the seeds. Cut into 3 cm pieces. Peel the pineapple and cut into small wedges. Peel and slice banana. Thinly slice star fruit.

3 Combine all fruit and syrup in large bowl, mixing gently. Cover and refrigerate for two hours before serving.

COOK'S FILE

Storage time: Tropical Fruit Salad is best eaten the day it is made.

Variation: Any fruits in season can be used for this dessert. Try exotic varieties such as jackfruit, guava or rambutans. Fruit should be of good quality, ripe but firm.

RASPBERRY AND STRAWBERRY JELLY

Preparation time: 30 minutes + 4 hours
   refrigeration
Total cooking time: Nil
Serves 8

250 g punnet strawberries,
   stalks removed
1 tablespoon sugar
250 g punnet raspberries
2 x 85 g packets strawberry or
   raspberry jelly crystals
1 cup boiling water
1 cup cold water
1 tablespoon lemon juice
whipped cream and chocolate
   curls, for decoration

➤ PROCESS STRAWBERRIES and
sugar until smooth. Pour mixture into
medium bowl.

1 Place the raspberries into a food
processor bowl. Process for 20–30
seconds or until smooth. Push the
mixture through a sieve. Add to the
strawberry mixture.

2 Combine jelly crystals and boiling
water in a large jug. Stir until dissolved. Add the berry mixture, cold
water and juice. Mix well (mixture
should equal 4 cups). Pour jelly into
individual dessert dishes or parfait
glasses. Refrigerate for 4 hours or
until set. Decorate with cream and
chocolate curls.

3 **To make chocolate curls:**
Chocolate curls can be easily made
using a vegetable peeler to shave the
flat side of a block of chocolate. For
best results, the chocolate should be
warmed so that it is easier to work
with, but not to the point where it is
beginning to melt (leave it in a warm
spot for 10 to 15 minutes). Working
over greaseproof paper, use long, even

strokes to shave chocolate. Spoon or
shake curls over jelly and cream.

COOK'S FILE

Storage time: Jelly may be made up
to 2 days ahead. Store in refrigerator.
Variation: Other berries, such as
loganberries or blackberries, can be

substituted for the raspberries or
strawberries, if desired. Jellies in cor-
responding flavours are available
from large supermarkets.

Jelly can also be poured into a flat
baking dish and chilled. When completely set, cut into cubes, pile into
individual dessert dishes and decorate
as desired.

FROZEN HONEY AND WHISKY LOG WITH RHUBARB SAUCE

Preparation time: 40 minutes
Total cooking time: 5–10 minutes
Serves 10–12

6 egg yolks
1/2 cup honey
1/4 cup whisky
2 1/2 cups cream,
  whipped

Rhubarb Sauce
750 g rhubarb, chopped
1 tablespoon grated orange rind
1 cup orange juice
1 1/4 cups sugar
1/2 cup water
pinch cinnamon

➤ LINE LOAF TIN 22 x 11 x 6.5 cm with foil.

1 Beat yolks with electric beaters until thick and pale. Heat honey in microwave oven on High for 15 seconds; or place in a jug and stand in bowl of hot water for 1 minute. Gradually add honey to egg yolks, beating constantly. Fold through whisky and cream. Pour into prepared tin. Freeze for 3–4 hours or until set.

2 To make Rhubarb Sauce: Place rhubarb, rind, juice, sugar, water and cinnamon in a pan and cook over medium heat until rhubarb is soft. Push the mixture through a sieve. Refrigerate sauce until cold.

3 Remove log from tin. Using a sharp knife, cut into slices and serve with rhubarb sauce.

COOK'S FILE

Storage time: Make the frozen loaf up to 1 week in advance. Sauce can be made 2 days ahead.

APPLE AND SULTANA BRANDIED BREAD PUDDING

Preparation time: 40 minutes
Total cooking time: 50–55 minutes
Serves 8–10

4 large green apples
1/2 cup water
1/3 cup caster sugar
1/2 cup sultanas
6 slices white bread
31/2 cups milk
1 teaspoon vanilla essence
2 tablespoons brandy
5 eggs

1/2 cup sugar, extra
nutmeg

➤ PREHEAT OVEN to moderate 180°C. Peel, core and chop the apples. Place in a medium pan.

1 Add water and sugar. Stir over low heat until sugar has dissolved. Cook 5–10 minutes or until apple is soft and liquid has reduced. Add the sultanas and remove from heat.

2 Cut bread, including the crusts, into small cubes. Place in a medium bowl. Add the milk, essence and brandy; leave to stand 10 minutes.

3 Beat eggs and sugar together. Carefully stir into the bread mixture. Place apple mixture in the base of square or round 9-cup capacity oven-proof dish. Spoon bread and egg mixture over the top of the apple and sprinkle with nutmeg. Place dish in a large baking dish, pour in enough water to come halfway up the sides. Place in oven and bake 45–50 minutes or until lightly set. Serve warm with cream or ice-cream.

COOK'S FILE

Storage time: Cook the pudding just before serving.
Hint: Substitute currants or chopped raisins for the sultanas, if desired. In place of the apples, pears, or a combination of half apples and half pears may be used.

LEMON PASSIONFRUIT SYLLABUB WITH BERRIES

Preparation time: 40 minutes
Total cooking time: Nil
Serves 10

2 teaspoons grated lemon rind
1/3 cup lemon juice
1/2 cup caster sugar
1/2 cup dry white wine
8 passionfruit
2 cups cream
2 x 250 g punnets blueberries

2 x 250 g punnets raspberries
2 tablespoons icing sugar
2 x 250 g punnets strawberries, stalks removed

➤ COMBINE RIND, juice, sugars and white wine in a jug; stir. Leave to stand for 10 minutes.

1 Cut four of the passionfruit in half. Push the pulp through a sieve to remove pips. Add passionfruit juice to the sugar and wine mixture.

2 Beat cream with electric beaters until it holds stiff peaks. Gradually beat in lemon and passionfruit syrup until all syrup is added (mixture will have the consistency of softly whipped cream). Add pulp, with pips removed, of remaining four passionfruit. Cover mixture and refrigerate for 1 hour.

3 Combine the blueberries, raspberries and sugar. Place mixture into a 7-cup capacity serving bowl. Spoon cream mixture over top of the berries. Decorate syllabub with strawberries, dust with icing sugar and serve.

COOK'S FILE

Storage time: Syllabub is a very light dessert and is best eaten within 12 hours of making.

*Opposite: Apple Bread Pudding (top),
Lemon and Passionfruit Syllabub (bottom)*

RICH CHOCOLATE BERRY LAYER CAKE

Preparation time: 20 minutes
Total cooking time: 1 hour–1 hour 15 minutes
Serves 12

125 g butter, chopped
1¼ cups sugar
3 eggs
1 cup plain flour
1 cup self-raising flour
²/₃ cup cocoa powder
½ cup water
½ cup thickened cream
½ cup milk

Filling
½ cup strawberry jam
1¼ cup cream, whipped
250 g punnet strawberries quartered

Icing
250 g unsalted butter
250 g dark cooking chocolate, chopped

➤ PREHEAT OVEN to moderately slow 160°C. Grease and line deep 23 cm round cake tin with baking paper.

1 Combine all cake ingredients in large bowl of electric mixer. Beat on low speed until mixture is combined, then beat on medium/high speed 3 minutes or until mixture is smooth and lighter in colour. Pour into prepared tin, bake 1–1¼ hours or until skewer comes out clean when inserted in cake. Stand cake in tin 5 minutes before turning onto wire rack to cool.

2 To make Filling: Cut cake into 3 layers horizontally. Place bottom cake layer on a serving plate, spread with half the jam. Spread with half each of cream and berries. Place another cake layer on top and repeat process with remaining jam, cream and berries. Top with remaining cake layer.

3 To make Icing: Melt butter in pan, add chocolate; remove from heat and let stand for 5 minutes. Stir until smooth and chocolate is melted. Cool icing mixture until it has reached a spreadable consistency. Spread over top and sides of cake, swirl icing on top, decorate with a strawberry.

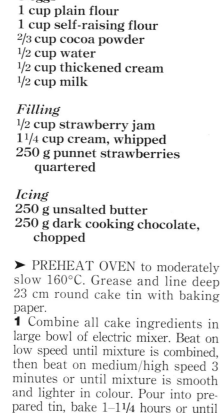

COOK'S FILE

Storage time: Best eaten on the day made; assemble several hours ahead.

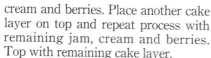
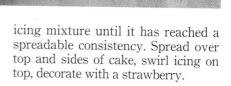

APRICOT AND APPLE NUT CRUMBLE

Preparation time: 30 minutes
Total cooking time: 25 minutes
Serves 6

425 g can apricot halves, drained
425 g can pie apple
1/4 cup hazelnuts, roughly chopped
1/4 cup pecans, roughly chopped
2 tablespoons almonds, roughly chopped

1/3 cup soft brown sugar
1/2 teaspoon ground cinnamon
2 tablespoons plain flour
3/4 cup breadcrumbs (made from stale bread)
1 tablespoon desiccated coconut
75 g unsalted butter, melted
1/4 teaspoon nutmeg

➤ PREHEAT OVEN to moderate 180°C. Brush a 23 cm square (or round) 5 cm high ovenproof dish with oil or melted butter.

1 Cut apricot pieces in half. Spread apple over the base of prepared dish. Follow with a layer of apricot halves, placed cut-side down.

2 Combine nuts, sugar, cinnamon, flour, breadcrumbs, coconut and melted butter, mix well. Spread evenly over fruit. Sprinkle with nutmeg.

3 Bake for 25 minutes or until top is golden and fruit hot. Serve hot or cold with whipped cream or custard.

COOK'S FILE

Storage time: Prepare mixture several hours in advance. Spread topping over crumble just before baking. Serve immediately after baking.

Hint: Any variety of canned fruit is suitable for this recipe.

FRUIT FLAN

Preparation time: 40 minutes
Total cooking time: 30 minutes
Makes 2 x 23 cm flans

Pastry
2¹/2 cups plain flour
¹/4 cup sugar
180 g butter, chopped
1 egg
1 egg yolk
1 tablespoon water

Custard
2¹/2 cups milk
3 eggs
2 tablespoons plain flour
2 tablespoons cornflour
¹/2 cup caster sugar
2 teaspoons vanilla essence

Topping
2 kiwi fruit, sliced
425 g can peach halves, sliced
14 black grapes
1 punnet strawberries, halved
¹/2 cup strawberry jam
1 tablespoon brandy

➤ PREHEAT OVEN to moderately hot 210°C.

1 To make Pastry: Place flour, sugar and butter in bowl of a food processor. Using the pulse action, process for 30 seconds or until the mixture is fine and crumbly. Add egg, egg yolk and the water and process for 20 seconds or until the mixture just comes together when squeezed. Turn onto a lightly floured board and knead gently to form a smooth dough. Refrigerate, covered with plastic wrap for 20 minutes. Halve pastry, wrap 1 portion in plastic wrap and set aside. Roll other half on a floured board large enough to fit a 23 cm round loose-bottomed flan tin. Ease pastry into the tin and trim edge with a sharp knife. Repeat with remaining half of pastry and a second flan tin. Cut a sheet of baking paper to cover each pastry-lined tin. Place the paper into each tin, spread a layer of dried beans or rice evenly on top. Bake for 10 minutes. Remove paper and rice or beans, bake for another 10 minutes or until lightly browned; cool.

2 To make Custard: Whisk ¹/2 cup milk with eggs, sifted flours and sugar in medium bowl. Heat remaining milk in a pan until warm, remove from heat and gradually whisk into egg mixture. Return the custard mixture to pan; whisk over heat until mixture boils and thickens. Simmer for 3 minutes. Stir in the essence. Remove from heat and cool. Spread into pastry case.

3 To make Topping: Arrange fruit decoratively over custard. Heat jam and brandy together in pan, then strain through a sieve. Brush over fruit. Refrigerate flan before serving.

COOK'S FILE

Storage time: Make flan several hours in advance.

CHERRY CHEESE STRUDEL

Preparation time: 25 minutes
Total cooking time: 35–40 minutes
Serves 8–10

500 g ricotta cheese
2 teaspoons orange or lemon rind
1/4 cup sugar
1/2 cup breadcrumbs
2 tablespoons ground almonds
2 eggs
425 g can stoneless black
    cherries
2 teaspoons cornflour
8 sheets filo pastry

60 g butter, melted
2 tablespoons packaged dry
    breadcrumbs
icing sugar

➤ PREHEAT OVEN to moderate 180°C. Lightly grease a baking tray with melted butter.

1 Combine cheese, rind, sugar, crumbs and almonds in a bowl. Add eggs; mix well. Drain cherries, reserving half the juice. Blend cornflour with reserved cherry juice in a small pan. Stir over heat until the mixture boils and thickens. Cool slightly.

2 Layer pastry sheets, brushing between each sheet with melted butter and sprinkling with a few breadcrumbs. Form a large square by placing second sheet halfway down the first sheet. Alternate layers, brushing with melted butter and sprinkling with breadcrumbs.

3 Place cheese mixture along one long edge of pastry. Shape into a log. Top with cherries and cooled syrup. Roll pastry around cheese filling, folding in edges as you roll. End with pastry edge underneath. Place on prepared tray. Bake for 35–40 minutes or until pastry is golden. Serve strudel warm or cold, heavily dusted with icing sugar. Cut into slices.

COOK'S FILE

Storage: Strudel can be made several hours in advance. It is best eaten on the day it is made.

CAKES

SOUR CREAM CHOCOLATE CAKE WITH RASPBERRY SAUCE

Preparation time: 35–40 minutes
Total cooking time: 35–40 minutes
Makes one 23 cm round cake

1/3 cup cocoa powder
1/3 cup boiling water
60 g unsalted butter
3/4 cup caster sugar
1 egg
1 teaspoon vanilla essence
1/2 teaspoon bicarbonate of soda
1/2 cup sour cream
1 cup plain flour

Ganache
150 g dark chocolate, chopped
1/2 cup cream

Raspberry Sauce
1–2 tablespoons caster sugar
2 x 250 punnets raspberries

➤ PREHEAT OVEN to moderate 180°C. Brush a shallow 23 cm round cake tin with oil or melted butter. Line base and sides of the tin with baking paper.
1 Sift cocoa into small mixing bowl. Pour in water; mix to form a smooth paste; cool. Using electric beaters, beat the butter and sugar in a small bowl until combined. Add egg and beat until light and creamy. Add essence and beat until combined. Transfer mixture to a large bowl. Combine soda and sour cream. Stir into the cocoa mixture. Add cocoa mixture to the creamed butter alternately with sifted flour. Beat until smooth. Pour mixture into prepared tin; smooth surface. Bake 35–40 minutes or until skewer comes out clean when inserted into the centre. Stand cake in tin for 5 minutes before turning out onto a wire rack to cool.
2 To make Ganache: Combine chocolate and cream in small pan. Stir over low heat until chocolate has melted and mixture is smooth. Remove from heat; cool. Place cake on wire rack set over a baking tray. Pour Ganache to completely cover the cake. Smooth top and sides and sides with a flat-bladed knife. Allow to set.
3 To make Raspberry Sauce: Place sugar and two-thirds of the raspberries in food processor and process for 30 seconds or until smooth. Serve Sauce poured over wedges of cake. Decorate with remaining berries if desired.

COOK'S FILE

Storage Time: Make the cake up to 2 days in advance; store in airtight container in cool, dry place. Make sauce up to a day ahead and keep in refrigerator in an airtight container.
Variation: Add a tablespoon of fruit liqueur, such as kirsch or Cointreau, to the Raspberry Sauce.

MARBLED BLUEBERRY CAKE

Preparation time: 30 minutes
Total cooking time: 50–55 minutes
Makes one 20 cm round cake

1 tablespoon sugar
1¼ cups fresh blueberries
2 eggs
½ teaspoon vanilla essence
125 g butter, melted
1⅓ cups self-raising flour, sifted
½ cup caster sugar
2 tablespoons soft brown sugar
icing sugar, sifted, for dusting

➤ PREHEAT OVEN to moderate 180°C. Brush a 20 cm round spring-form tin with oil or melted butter. Line the base and sides with baking paper.

1 Place sugar and half the blueberries in medium pan. Stir gently over medium heat 1–2 minutes or until juices begin to run. Remove from heat. Stir in remaining berries, cool.

2 Beat eggs in a small mixing bowl. Add essence and butter, mix well. Combine flour and sugar in medium mixing bowl. Make a well in the centre. Using a metal spoon, stir in egg mixture until smooth.

3 Take out ¾ cup of cake mixture and stir into blueberries. Place spoon-

fuls of both mixtures randomly into prepared tin. Swirl mixture with a knife or skewer to produce a marbled effect. Sprinkle brown sugar over the top. Bake 45–50 minutes or until a skewer comes out clean when inserted into the centre. Stand cake in tin on wire rack to cool 5 minutes before removing. Serve cake dusted liberally with icing sugar, or decorate with extra berries and cream if desired.

COOK'S FILE

Storage time: This cake is best eaten on the day it is made.
Hint: Replace the blueberries with raspberries, if desired, or if blueberries are out of season.

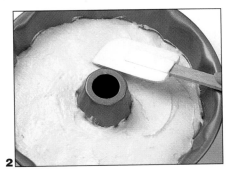

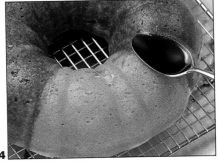

COFFEE COGNAC SYRUP CAKE

Preparation time: 45 minutes
Total cooking time: 45–50 minutes
Makes one 23 cm ring cake

185 g butter
3/4 cup caster sugar
3 eggs, separated
1 teaspoon grated lemon rind
1 cup sour cream
1/4 cup plain yoghurt
1 3/4 cups self-raising flour
1/4 cup ground almonds

Syrup
1 cup medium strong coffee
1/2 cup caster sugar
2 tablespoons cognac

➤ PREHEAT OVEN to moderate 180°C. Brush a 23 cm baba, fluted ring or savarin tin with oil or melted butter. Dust tin lightly with flour, shake off excess.

1 Using electric beaters, beat butter and sugar until light and creamy. Add egg yolks one at a time, beating thoroughly after each addition. Add rind and beat mixture until combined. Transfer to large mixing bowl. Add combined cream and yoghurt alternately with the sifted flour. Stir until combined and mixture is smooth. Stir in the almonds.

2 Beat the egg whites with electric beaters until stiff peaks form. Using a metal spoon, carefully fold egg whites into flour mixture. Spoon mixture into prepared tin, smoothing surface. Bake 5 minutes. Reduce oven temperature to moderately slow 160°C. Bake a further 35–40 minutes or until skewer comes out clean when inserted into the centre of cake. Stand cake in tin 5 minutes before turning onto a wire rack to cool.

3 To make Syrup: Combine coffee, sugar and cognac in small pan. Stir over low heat without boiling until sugar has dissolved. Bring to boil, reduce heat and simmer 2–3 minutes to reduce liquid. Remove pan from heat and cool mixture slightly.

4 Stand cake on wire rack over baking tray; skewer cake randomly on top. Spoon coffee cognac syrup over cake; collect excess syrup from baking tray and spoon over cake again. Cool cake completely. Decorate with piped, whipped cream and chocolate curls before serving.

COOK'S FILE

Storage time: Cake is best eaten on the day it is made.

ALMOND STICKY CAKE

Preparation time: 20 minutes
Total cooking time: 50 minutes
Makes one 23 cm round cake

4 eggs
3/4 cup caster sugar
2 teaspoons grated orange rind
90 g butter, melted
1/4 cup cream
3/4 cup self-raising flour

Almond Topping
2 cups flaked almonds
90 g butter
1/3 cup caster sugar
1/4 cup cream
2 tablespoons honey
1/2 teaspoon ground mixed spice

➤ PREHEAT OVEN to moderate 180°C.

1 Brush a deep 23 cm round spring-form tin with oil or melted butter. Line base and sides with baking paper.

2 Using electric beaters, beat eggs and sugar in a large mixing bowl until thick and pale. Using a metal spoon, fold in orange rind, butter and cream. Add sifted flour, fold in quickly and lightly. Pour mixture into prepared tin. Bake for 40 minutes or until cake is firm in the centre.

3 To make Almond Topping: Combine almonds, butter, sugar, cream, honey and mixed spice in a medium pan. Stir over medium heat until mixture boils.

4 Spread Almond Topping over top of cake and bake for another 10 minutes or until topping has turned golden. Leave cake in the tin to cool for 10 minutes before transferring to serving plate.

COOK'S FILE

Storage time: This cake is best eaten on the day of baking.

Hint: Due to the sticky nature of this cake, it is best to use specially coated-baking paper to line the springform tin, rather than greaseproof paper. Serve the cake with a bowl of cream or custard for guests to help themselves. Cake can be served warm or cold, and makes a great morning or afternoon tea treat.

LEMON CREAM CAKE

Preparation time: 20 minutes
Total cooking time: 20 minutes
Makes one 20 cm round cake

1/3 cup cornflour
1/3 cup plain flour
1/3 cup self-raising flour
4 eggs
2/3 cup caster sugar
2 teaspoons grated lemon rind

Lemon Cream
1 1/2 cups cream
1/3 cup lemon butter
1/2 cup halved pecans

➤PREHEAT OVEN to moderate 180°C. Brush 2 shallow, 20 cm round cake tins with oil or melted butter. Line base with baking paper; grease paper. Dust tins lightly with flour, shake off excess. Sift combined flours 3 times onto greaseproof paper.

1 Place eggs in large mixing bowl. Using electric beaters, beat for 5 minutes or until thick and pale. Add the sugar gradually, beating constantly until dissolved. Using a metal spoon, fold in the lemon rind and flours quickly and lightly.

2 Spread mixture evenly in prepared tins. Bake 20 minutes or until lightly golden. Stand cakes 2 minutes before turning onto a wire rack to cool.

3 To make Lemon Cream: Beat cream and lemon butter in a small bowl with electric beaters until soft peaks form. Cut each cake in half horizontally. Place one layer on a serving plate, spread with a quarter of the lemon cream. Continue layering with remaining cake and lemon cream, icing top of cake with lemon cream as well. Sprinkle with pecans and serve.

COOK'S FILE

Storage time: This cake is best eaten on the day of baking. It can be assembled several hours ahead and stored in the refrigerator.
Variation: Decorate with walnuts or chopped pistachios, of preferred.

1

2

3

BLACK FOREST CAKE

Preparation time: 1 hour +
30 minutes standing
Total cooking time: 50–60 minutes
Makes one 20 cm round cake

125 g butter
1 cup caster sugar
2 eggs, lightly beaten
1 teaspoon vanilla essence
1/3 cup self-raising flour
1 cup plain flour
1 teaspoon bicarbonate
   of soda
1/2 cup cocoa powder
3/4 cup buttermilk

Filling
1/4 cup cherry liqueur
3 cups cream, whipped
425 g can pitted cherries,
   drained

Topping
100 g block dark chocolate
100 g block milk chocolate
fresh cherries or maraschino
   cherries with stalks,
   for decoration

➤ PREHEAT OVEN to moderate 180°C. Brush a deep, 20 cm round cake tin with oil or melted butter. Line base and sides with baking paper.

1 Using electric beaters, beat the butter and sugar until light and creamy. Add eggs gradually, beating well after each addition. Add vanilla essence and beat until combined. Transfer the mixture to a large mixing bowl. Using a metal spoon, fold in the sifted flours, soda and cocoa alternately with the buttermilk. Stir until combined and the mixture is smooth.

2 Pour mixture into the prepared tin; smooth surface. Bake for 50–60 minutes or until a skewer comes out clean when inserted into the centre of the cake. Let cake stand in the tin for 30 minutes before turning it out onto a wire rack to cool.

3 When cold, cut cake into three layers horizontally. Brush surface of cake layers liberally with cherry liqueur.

4 To assemble cake: Place one cake layer on a serving plate. Spread evenly with one fifth of the whipped cream. Top with half the cherries.

Continue layering with the remaining cake, cherries and cream, finishing with the cream. Spread the cream evenly around the outside of the cake. Coat side with chocolate shavings. Pipe rosettes of cream around the top edge of the cake and decorate with fresh or maraschino cherries on stalks and more chocolate shavings.

5 To make Chocolate Shavings: Leave chocolate blocks in a warm place 10–15 minutes or until chocolate is soft but still firm. With a vegetable peeler, and using long strokes, shave curls of chocolate from the side of the block. Refrigerate to harden, if necessary.

COOK'S FILE

Storage time: The cake can be made up to a day ahead. Assemble just before serving. Chocolate shavings can be prepared 2–3 days beforehand and stored in an airtight container in a cool, dry place, or in the refrigerator.

Hint: Cherry liqueur, or kirsch, is a colourless liqueur available from most liquor shops. Cherry brandy is a dark liqueur and can be substituted for kirsch.

Variation: The traditional version of Black Forest Cake, one of the world's best known celebratory cakes, uses fresh Morello cherries, where available, for the filling. If using fresh cherries, poach them first in a sugar syrup before removing the stones. Drain before using to fill cake.

Decorate the side of the cake with toasted, flaked almonds in place of the chocolate shavings, if desired. Scoop nuts into the side of your hand and gently press around the side of the cake. Alternatively, decorate the top of the cake with chocolate curls dusted with icing sugar.

The cake can also be served simply with your favourite icing.

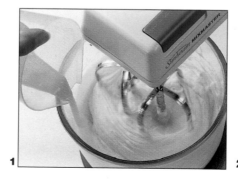

1

2

3

4

5

COFFEE NIBBLES

RASPBERRY CREAM MERINGUES

Preparation time: 40 minutes
Total cooking time: 20–30 minutes
Makes 50

2 egg whites
1/2 cup caster sugar
2 teaspoons cornflour
1 teaspoon lime or lemon juice

Raspberry Cream
100 g cream cheese
55 g white chocolate, melted
2 tablespoons sour cream
2 teaspoons icing sugar
1/4 cup cream, whipped
100 g raspberries, lightly
   crushed
white chocolate shavings, extra,
   for decoration

➤ PREHEAT OVEN to slow 150°C.
Line two oven trays with baking
paper.
1 Place egg whites in small dry mixing bowl. Using electric beaters, beat
until soft peaks form. Add sugar
gradually, beating constantly until
mixture is thick and glossy and all
the sugar has dissolved. Add cornflour and juice beat until combined.
2 Spoon meringue mixture into a piping bag fitted with a 7 mm fluted star
nozzle. Pipe meringue mixture onto
trays in small 2–3 cm round nests.
Bake 20–30 minutes or until pale and
crisp. Turn oven off. Cool meringues
completely on tray in oven, with door
slightly ajar. Remove when cool and
fill with Raspberry Cream. Decorate
with white chocolate shavings.
3 To make Raspberry Cream:
Using electric beaters, beat cream
cheese until light and creamy. Add
white chocolate, beat until smooth.
Add sour cream and sugar; beat until
well combined. Using a metal spoon,
fold in cream and raspberries.

COOK'S FILE

Storage time: Make meringue nests
up to a week in advance. Store in an
airtight container in a cool, dry place.
Fill just before serving as meringues
will soften if filled too early .
Variation: These meringue nests
can be made larger and served,
topped with fresh raspberries, as a
dessert. Use strawberries, blackberries or blueberries instead of raspberries to make filling, if desired.
Meringues are also great filled with
fresh mango.

ORANGE AND ALMOND TUILES

Preparation time: 10 minutes
Total cooking time: 10 minutes
Makes about 15

90 g butter
1/3 cup caster sugar
1/4 cup plain flour
1/4 cup flaked almonds, crushed
  slightly
1 tablespoon finely chopped
  mixed peel

➤ PREHEAT OVEN to moderate 180°C. Brush a large oven tray with oil or melted butter and dust lightly with flour.

1 Using electric beaters, beat butter and sugar in a small mixing bowl until light and creamy. Add flour and stir until combined. Add the almonds and peel; stir until combined.

2 Cook tuiles in batches. Place heaped teaspoonfuls of the mixture about 10 cm apart on the prepared tray. Spread each spoonful of the mixture out into a 5 cm circle. Bake for 10 minutes or until brown.

3 Remove trays from oven; stand for 1 minute. Carefully lift each circle in turn off the tray with a spatula and drape it immediately over a rolling pin to curl. Allow to cool on rolling pin. Repeat with remaining circles.

COOK'S FILE

Storage time: Tuiles can be stored in an airtight container for several days before use.

Hint: Cook only about 4–6 tuiles at a time, as they cool and harden very quickly. Grease and flour the tray again before baking each batch.

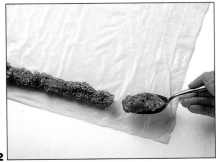

HAZELNUT AND HONEY COIL

Preparation time: 30 minutes
Total cooking time: 25 minutes
Makes one 18 cm coil

Filling
1 cup hazelnuts, finely ground
³/4 cup icing sugar
30 g butter
2 tablespoons orange juice
¹/2 teaspoon ground cinnamon
1 egg yolk

4 sheets filo pastry
60 g butter, melted
2 tablespoons honey
1 tablespoon chopped hazelnuts

➤ PREHEAT OVEN to moderate 180°C. Brush an oven tray with oil or melted butter.

1 To make Filling: Combine ground hazelnuts, icing sugar, butter, orange juice and cinnamon in a medium pan. Stir over low heat for 5 minutes or until mixture forms a ball. Remove from heat. Add egg yolk and stir quickly until combined; cool.

2 Lay a sheet of filo pastry on work surface and brush with melted butter. Top with another sheet of pastry, brush with butter. Spoon half the filling evenly along the long side of the pastry, roll it up to enclose filling; brush with butter. Repeat with remaining pastry and filling. Brush rolls with half the honey.

3 Curl one of the rolls firmly into a flattened coil shape. Attach remaining roll to the end of the coil by tucking one end inside the end of the first coil. Continue curling to produce one large coil; tuck end under to seal.

4 Place coil on prepared tray. Brush with honey and sprinkle with chopped hazelnuts. Bake for 20–25 minutes or until golden brown. Cool. Cut coil into wedges to serve.

COOK'S FILE

Storage time: Hazelnut and Honey Coil can be cooked a day in advance. Store in an airtight container.

Variation: Other nuts, such as almonds, pistachios or walnuts, or a mixture of nuts, can be used instead of hazelnuts to make the filling.

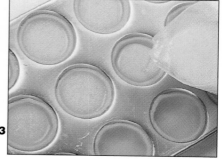

LEMON AND PASSIONFRUIT TARTLETS

Preparation time: 15 minutes +
15 minutes refrigeration
Total cooking time: 20 minutes
Makes 24

Shortcrust Pastry
1¹/2 cups plain flour
90 g butter, chopped
2 egg yolks
1-2 tablespoons iced water
pulp of 1 passionfruit
2 eggs, lightly beaten
¹/3 cup caster sugar
¹/3 cup lemon juice
2 tablespoons cream
60 g white chocolate melts

➤ PREHEAT OVEN to moderately hot 210°C (Gas 190°C). Brush two 12-cup shallow patty tins with melted butter.

1 Place flour and butter in food processor bowl. Process for 20 seconds or until mixture is fine and crumbly. Add egg yolk and almost all the water, process for 20 seconds or until mixture comes together, adding more water if necessary. Turn onto lightly floured surface and form into a smooth ball. Cover and refrigerate pastry for 15 minutes. Roll pastry between 2 sheets of baking paper to a thickness of 3 mm. Cut rounds using a 6.5 cm plain or fluted cutter. Ease pastry rounds into prepared tins.

2 Push passionfruit pulp through a sieve. Combine juice in a jug with eggs, sugar, lemon juice and cream.

3 Pour the mixture into tartlet cases. Place in oven, reduce heat to slow 150°C and bake for 10 minutes or until just set. Remove from oven; cool.

4 Place chocolate in a small heatproof bowl. Stand bowl over a pan of simmering water and stir until chocolate has melted and is smooth. Spoon into a small paper icing bag; seal the open end. Snip tip off the icing bag and drizzle chocolate in a lattice pattern over tartlets.

COOK'S FILE

Storage time: Tartlets are best eaten the day they are made.
Variation: Milk chocolate melts can be used for drizzling, if desired.
Hint: Use two 275 g packets of sweet shortcrust tart cases, if time is short.

SUGAR 'N' SPICE WALNUTS

Preparation time: 5 minutes
Total cooking time: 8 minutes
Serves 8

60 g butter
1 teaspoon ground cinnamon
1 teaspoon ground cardamom
2 cups walnut halves

1/4 cup caster sugar

➤ PREHEAT OVEN to moderately hot 210°C (Gas 190°C).

1 Melt butter in a medium pan; remove from heat. Add cinnamon and cardamom; stir until combined.

2 Add the walnuts and stir until well coated in spice mixture. Spread walnuts in a single layer on an oven tray. Bake for 8 minutes or until lightly browned; remove from oven.

3 Place sugar in a medium bowl. Add the hot walnuts and stir until well coated. Serve hot or cold.

COOK'S FILE

Storage time: Cooked walnuts can be stored in an airtight container in a cool place for several days.

Variation: Pecans, which are closely related to walnuts, may be used in this recipe, or use a mixture of other nuts if desired.

FROSTED CRESCENTS

Preparation time: 50 minutes
Total cooking time: 12 minutes
Makes 50

**60 g roasted macadamia nuts
 or almonds
1 cup plain flour
¼ cup sugar
½ teaspoon grated orange rind
125 g butter, chopped
1 egg yolk
icing sugar for dusting**

➤ PREHEAT OVEN to moderate 180°C. Brush two oven trays with oil or melted butter. Place macadamia nuts or almonds in a food processor bowl. Process until finely crushed.

1 Sift flour in medium bowl; add sugar, rind and butter. Using fingertips, rub butter into flour mixture for 5 minutes, or until mixture is fine and crumbly. Add egg yolk and ground nuts. Mix to form a soft dough.

2 Shape level teaspoonfuls of mixture into small crescents and place on prepared trays. Bake for 12 minutes or until pale golden in colour.

3 While crescents are still warm, sift a generous amount of icing sugar over them. Stand crescents for 2 minutes. Transfer to wire racks to cool completely.

COOK'S FILE

Storage time: Prepare crescents up to 1 week in advance. Store in an airtight container in a cool, dry place.

Variation: Use lemon rind in place of orange rind, if desired. Add a quarter to half a teaspoonful of orange-flower water or rosewater to the dough for extra flavour.

PISTACHIO PRALINE TRUFFLES

Preparation time: 50 minutes
+ refrigeration
Total cooking time: 15–20 minutes
Makes 55

1/3 cup shelled pistachio nuts
1/2 cup sugar
1/4 cup water
45 g unsalted butter, chopped
250 g dark chocolate, chopped
1/3 cup cream
2 teaspoons brandy or cognac
1/3 cup cocoa powder, sifted

► PREHEAT OVEN to moderate 180°C. Place the shelled pistachios in a shallow cake tin. Bake 5–10 minutes or until the nuts are lightly roasted. Remove from oven and cool.

1 Combine sugar and water in medium pan. Stir over low heat without boiling until sugar has dissolved. Brush sugar crystals from side of pan with a wet pastry brush. Bring to boil, reduce heat, simmer for 8–10 minutes or until syrup turns golden. Remove from heat. Stir in nuts. Pour mixture onto an oiled, foil-lined tray; cool.

2 Place butter and chocolate in medium heatproof bowl. Stand bowl over pan of simmering water and stir until mixture has melted and is smooth. Remove from heat; cool slightly. Add cream and brandy, mix well; cool.

3 Place cold, hardened toffee in a plastic freezer bag; using a meat mallet or rolling pin, finely crush toffee. Add to chocolate mixture, mix well. Cover and refrigerate for 45 minutes or until mixture is firm enough to handle.

4 Roll teaspoonfuls of mixture into small balls. Place on a paper-lined tray and refrigerate for 15 minutes. Roll in sifted cocoa and serve.

COOK'S FILE

Storage time: Make truffles up to a week in advance. Store in an airtight container, between layers of grease-proof paper, in the refrigerator.

ORANGE CHOCOLATE DATES

Preparation time: 50 minutes
Total cooking time: 5–10 minutes
Makes 24

12 small fresh dates
2/3 cup ground almonds
1 teaspoon grated orange rind
2 tablespoons icing sugar
2 teaspoons kirsch or Cointreau
2 teaspoons orange juice
2 oranges
1/2 cup caster sugar
1/4 cup water
250 g dark chocolate melts,
    melted (for dipping)
60 g milk chocolate melts, melted
    (for drizzling)

➤ CUT DATES in half lengthways; remove and discard stones.

1 Combine almonds, rind, sugar and liqueur in a small bowl. Add enough juice to form a moist mixture. Stir until well combined.

2 Divide the mixture into 24 portions. Roll each into a sausage shape, place lengthways down centre of each date.

3 Using a vegetable peeler, peel away the rind from both oranges, avoiding the white pith. Cut into long thin strips, using a sharp knife. Combine rind, sugar and water in small pan. Stir over low heat for 3 minutes or until sugar dissolves. Simmer uncovered, without stirring, for 5 minutes. Lift rind onto a wire rack to drain.

4 To Dip Dates in Chocolate: Place melted dark chocolate in small bowl. Using a fork, dip dates one at a time into the chocolate. Lift out, drain excess and place on a foil-lined tray. Drizzle with melted milk chocolate and decorate with candied rind while chocolate is still wet.

To Drizzle Dates with Chocolate: Place melted milk chocolate in small paper icing bag, seal open end, snip off tip. Pipe chocolate back and forth along each date.

COOK'S FILE

Storage time: Prepare dates up to 2 weeks in advance. Store in an airtight container in the refrigerator.
Hint: Add 5–10 g white vegetable shortening to chocolate if too thick.

CHOCOLATE BUTTER FINGERS

Preparation time: 30 minutes
Total cooking time: 15 minutes
Makes 40

125 g butter
1/3 cup icing sugar
1/2 teaspoon vanilla essence
1/2 teaspoon grated lemon rind
1 teaspoon cream
1/2 cup cornflour
1/2 cup plain flour
60 g chocolate melts, melted

➤ PREHEAT OVEN to moderate 180°C. Brush two oven trays with oil or melted butter; line with baking paper.

1 Using electric beaters, beat butter and sugar until light and creamy. Add essence, rind and cream, beat until combined. Add sifted flours. Beat until mixture is smooth enough for piping.

2 Spoon mixture into a piping bag fitted with a 1.5 cm star nozzle. Pipe 4 cm lengths onto prepared trays. Bake for 15 minutes or until lightly golden. Cool fingers on trays before transferring to wire rack.

3 Place melted chocolate in a small paper icing bag, seal open end, snip off tip. Drizzle chocolate diagonally over fingers. Allow to set. Serve.

COOK'S FILE

Storage time: Biscuits can be made up to 3 days in advance. Store in an airtight container in cool, dark place.
Variation: Decorate biscuits with dark or white chocolate, or dust with combined icing sugar and cocoa.
Hint: When melting chocolate, take care not to let water come into contact with melting mixture or it will begin to seize and harden immediately.

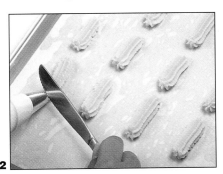

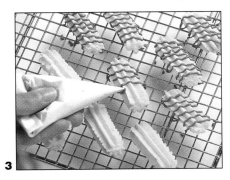

CHOCOLATE FRUIT ROUNDS

Preparation time: 30 minutes +
  12 hours refrigeration
Total cooking time: 5 minutes
Makes 50–60

1/3 cup blanched almonds
125 g dried apricots
1/2 cup (90 g) sultanas
1/3 cup (60 g) mixed peel
60 g unsalted butter
1/3 cup cream
250 g dark chocolate, chopped
1/3 cup (60 g) currants

1 tablespoon brandy or Grand
  Marnier
1 1/2 cups pecan nuts or walnuts

➤ PREHEAT OVEN to moderate 180°C. Place almonds on baking tray. Bake 5–10 minutes or until golden. Cool and chop finely. Finely chop the apricots, sultanas and mixed peel.

1 Place butter and cream in a small pan. Stir over low heat until butter has melted and mixture is almost boiling; remove from heat. Pour mixture over chocolate in a medium mixing bowl. Stir with a wooden spoon until chocolate has melted and mixture is smooth.

2 Add almonds, fruits and brandy, mix well. Cover and refrigerate 2–3 hours or until firm enough to handle.

3 Divide mixture into 5 equal portions. Roll each into a thin sausage shape, 2 cm in diameter. Roll logs in finely chopped pecans or walnuts. Wrap in plastic wrap and refrigerate for 12 hours or overnight. Using a sharp, flat-bladed knife, cut logs into 1.5 cm wide rounds.

COOK'S FILE

Storage time: Rounds can be made up to 2 weeks in advance and stored, unsliced and wrapped in plastic, or frozen for up to 6 weeks.

CARAMEL CREAM CUPS

Preparation time: 40 minutes
Total cooking time: 10–15 minutes
Makes 30

60 g dark chocolate melts
30 foil confectionery cups
200 g jersey caramels, roughly
   chopped
40 g butter
2 tablespoons cream
1 tablespoon crème de cacao
cocoa powder, for dusting
50 g milk chocolate
   melts, for drizzling

➤ PLACE DARK chocolate melts in a small heatproof bowl. Stand bowl over a pan of simmering water, stir until the chocolate has melted and is smooth. Remove from heat.

1 Working with one at a time, pour a teaspoon of melted chocolate into each confectionery cup. Use a small brush to coat the cup thickly and evenly, making sure there are no gaps. Turn case upside down on a wire rack to set.

2 Combine caramels, butter, cream and crème de cacao in a small pan. Stir over low heat for 3–4 minutes or until caramels have melted. Remove from heat, beat until smooth; cool slightly.

3 Spoon caramel mixture into each chocolate cup. Allow caramel to set (cups may need refrigerating for 10–15 minutes if the weather is warm). Serve cups dusted with cocoa, or drizzled with milk chocolate.

COOK'S FILE

Storage time: Caramel Cream Cups will keep for up to 2 weeks in a container in a cool, dry place.

Variation: White or milk chocolate can be used in place of dark chocolate to make cups. Extra chocolate can also be melted and spooned on top of caramel cups. Allow to set, then carefully peel away foil cups and serve.

1

2

3

HAZELNUT COFFEE BISCUITS

Preparation time: 1 hour + 20 minutes
 refrigeration
Total cooking time: 25–30 minutes
Makes 50–60

125 g butter
1/2 cup caster sugar
1 teaspoon grated lemon rind
1 egg yolk
1 teaspoon lemon juice
1 cup (125 g) hazelnuts, ground
1 1/4 cups plain flour

Icing
1 cup icing sugar
30 g unsalted butter, melted
3–4 teaspoons lemon juice

Coffee Cream
1/2 cup sugar
1/4 cup water
1 tablespoon instant coffee
 powder
80 g unsalted butter

➤ PREHEAT OVEN to moderate 180°C. Line two oven trays with baking paper.

1 Beat butter and sugar with electric beaters until light and creamy. Add rind, egg yolk, juice and nuts, beat until well combined. Using a metal spoon, stir in sifted flour. Form mixture into a smooth ball. Wrap in plastic wrap and refrigerate for 15–20 minutes. Divide mixture in half. Roll one portion between two sheets of baking paper to a thickness of 4 mm. Cut out rounds using 3 cm fluted cutter. Place rounds on prepared tray. Repeat with remaining dough. Bake for 10 minutes or until biscuits are lightly golden. Remove from oven and transfer to wire racks to cool.

To make Icing: Combine sifted icing sugar, butter and enough lemon juice to form a smooth mixture. Place into a small paper piping bag, snip off tip. Pipe a tight spiral of icing onto each biscuit.

2 To make Coffee Cream: Combine sugar, water and coffee powder in a small pan. Stir over low heat, without boiling, until sugar has dissolved. Bring to boil, reduce heat and simmer, uncovered, without stirring

for 4–5 minutes. Beat butter until light and creamy. Pour cooled syrup in a thin stream onto the butter, beating constantly until thick and glossy.

3 Place into a small paper piping bag, snip off tip to an inverted 'V'. Pipe small rosettes on top of iced biscuits.

COOK'S FILE

Storage time: Make up to a week in advance and store, un-iced, in an airtight container in a cool, dry place.

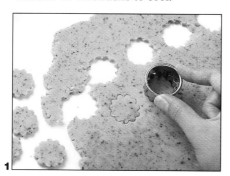

INDEX

USEFUL INFORMATION

All our recipes are tested in the Australian Family Circle® Test Kitchen. Standard metric measuring cups and spoons approved by Standards Australia are used in the development of our recipes. All cup and spoon measurements are level. We have used 60 g (Grade 3) eggs in all recipes. Sizes of cans vary from manufacturer to manufacturer and between countries—use the can size closest to the one suggested in the recipe.

Conversion Guide

1 cup	= 250 ml (8 fl oz)
1 teaspoon	= 5 ml
1 Australian tablespoon	= 20 ml (4 teaspoons)
1 UK/US tablespoon	= 15 ml (3 teaspoons)

NOTE: We have used 20 ml tablespoon measures. If you are using a 15 ml tablespoon, for most recipes the difference will not be noticeable. However, for recipes using baking powder, gelatine, bicarbonate of soda, small amounts of flour and cornflour, add an extra teaspoon for each tablespoon specified.

Dry Measures

30 g	= 1 oz
250 g	= 8 oz
500 g	= 1 lb

Liquid Measures

30 ml	= 1 fl oz
125 ml	= 4 fl oz
250 ml	= 8 fl oz

Linear Measures

6 mm	= ¼ inch
1 cm	= ½ inch
2.5 cm	= 1 inch

Cup Conversions

1 cup soft breadcrumbs	= 80 g (2¾ oz)
1 cup coriander leaves	= 30 g (1 oz)
1 cup grated Cheddar cheese	= 125 g (4 oz)
1 cup grated mozzarella cheese	= 150 g (5 oz)
1 cup chopped peanuts	= 160 g (5¼ oz)
1 cup cooked short-grain rice	= 185 g (6 oz)
1 cup raw short-grain rice	= 220 g (7 oz)
1 cup desiccated coconut	= 90 g (3 oz)
1 cup caster sugar	= 250 g (8 oz)

Oven Temperatures

Cooking times may vary slightly depending on the type of oven you are using. Before you preheat the oven, we suggest that you refer to the manufacturer's instructions to ensure proper temperature control.

	°C	°F	Gas Mark
Very slow	120	250	½
Slow	150	300	2
Warm	170	325	3
Moderate	180	350	4
Mod. hot	190	375	5
Mod. hot	200	400	6
Hot	220	425	7
Very hot	230	450	8

NOTE: For fan-forced ovens check your appliance manual, but as a general rule, set oven temperature to 20°C lower than the temperature indicated in the recipe.

International Glossary

kumera	sweet potato
lavash bread	use pitta bread
green prawns	raw prawns
zucchini	courgette
Lebanese cucumber	use any cucumber
snow peas	mange tout
blade/skirt beef	chuck or braising steak

Published by Murdoch Books®, a division of Murdoch Magazines Pty Limited, GPO Box 1203, Sydney NSW 1045.

Managing Editor: Rachel Carter. **Food Editors:** Kerrie Ray, Tracy Rutherford, Jody Vassallo. **Editor:** Deirdre Blayney. **Designer:** Jackie Richards. **Recipe Development:** Tracey Port, Wendy Berecry, Jacki Passmore, Beverley Sutherland Smith. **Food Stylists:** Mary Harris, Rosemary De Santis, Suzi Smith. **Photographers:** Joe Filshie, Luis Martin, Peter Scott, Andre Martin, Reg Morrison (Steps). **Food Preparation:** Melanie McDermott, Tracey Port, Dimitra Stais, Maria Sampsonis, Anna Paola Boyd.

CEO & Publisher: Anne Wilson.

National Library of Australia Cataloguing-in-Publication Data. Party and finger food. Includes index. ISBN 0 86411 387 0. 1. Cookery. 2. Entertaining. 3. Snack foods. 641.568. First printed 1994. Reprinted 1996 (twice), 1997 (twice), 1998, 1999, 2000. Printed by Prestige Litho, Queensland. PRINTED IN AUSTRALIA